r. A. bentinck

The

Collection

r. A. bentinck

FYAPUBLISHING | GEORGETOWN

The *Seductive* Collection

Copyright © 2019 by **r. A. bentinck**

All rights reserved. No part of this publication may be reproduced, distributed, or transmitted in any form or by any means, without prior written permission.

FyaPublishing
95 South Turkeyen,
Georgetown, Guyana.

The  **Collection r. A bentinck**
ISBN: **978-0-9994445-5-9**

Cover design by r. A bentinck
Cover image by Taonesesa Tiwanna Karidza

FyaPublishing.
Self-Publishing Made Easy

CONTENTS

chapter one 1
   The Breakfast Table 3
   Fine Wine 5
   Hypnotic Eyes 6
   Intoxicated 7
   Just One Thought 8
   Kissing King 9
   Lazy Days 10
   Like Fine Wine 11
   Linger a Little Longer 12
   Morning Wish 13
   Romancing the Wine 14
   Flaming Desires 15
   Smile 16
   Smooth Jazz and Fine Wine 17
   Sunday Mornings 18
   The Aftermath 19
   The Little Things 20
   The Moon Smiles 21
   This World of Mine 22

The *Seductive* Collection

Time *23*
We Make Music *24*
Whispering Flowers *25*
Pillows and Sheets *26*
The Sweetness from Your Lips *27*
Naked *28*
Cooling Relief *29*
Expectations *30*
Making it Hard *31*
Curves *33*
Breezy Relief *34*
Desirable *35*
In Your Eyes *36*
Light Your Fire *37*
Signature Sounds *38*
Soaked *39*
The Shower *40*
Unlocked *41*
Against the Wall *42*
Late Night Dinner *43*
Her Pink Lingerie *44*
Feline Tendencies *45*
I Wanna *47*
I Wish *48*

r. A. bentinck

Impatient *49*
In My Mind *50*
Peaceful Sleep *51*
Pulsating Petals *52*
Salty Nectar *53*
She Said… *54*
Slow and Easy *55*
Suddenly *56*
Fantasies *57*
What You Gonna Do? *58*
Whatever *59*
Misinterpretation *61*
Don't Speak *62*
Your Embrace *63*
One More Time *64*
Just to Please *65*
The Teasing Game *66*
Unfulfilled Desires *67*
All Yours *68*
Finally *69*
Those Moments *70*
Led *71*
Roaming Tongue *72*
She is Unbelievable *73*

The Seductive Collection

In the Rain *74*
The Artist at Work *76*
Undressing *77*
Turning Petals *78*
Rhythms *79*
Waiting *80*
Unfinished *81*
Poetess *82*
Satisfaction *83*
In the Dark *84*
Glistening *85*
Chasing Flavours *86*
Doing Dishes *87*
Her *88*
One *89*
Picking Fruits *90*
Secrets *91*
Tell Me *92*
You're *93*
The Proclamation *94*
Instigating *95*
Let Me *96*
Dangerous *97*
Midnight *98*

r. A. bentinck

Touched	99
Transgressing Eyes	100
In this Moment	101
Tonight	102
Of all the Things	103
Velvet Screams	104
One Dance (Gingerbay Café)	105
Falling Clothes	107
Don't Make Me Wait	108
Fatal Whispers	109
Scented Trail	110
The Wild Side	111
Dirty Desires	112
Steamy	113
Unchained Desires	114
Risqué Roulette	115
Pillow Fight	116
On the Phone	117
Waking Me Up	118
I Love	119
On Those Days	120
Magical Fingers	121
Speechless	122
Lavish Longings	123

The *Seductive* Collection

Morning Ride *124*
Shower Exist *125*
Come Back, Baby *126*
Dreams *128*
Take Back *129*
Show Me the Way *130*
Rainy Days *131*
Whispers *132*
Give Me a Reason *133*
All Over Me *134*
Underneath the Sheets *135*
Drizzled Honey *136*
Reflection *137*
Fooling Around - Scene 1 .... *138*
Fooling Around - Scene 2 .... *139*
Fooling Around - Scene 3 .... *140*
P.M. Scenes *141*
Slow Surrender *142*
Unbuttoning *143*
Pretty Feet *144*
Lustful Longing *145*
Don't Stop *146*
Penetration *147*
Let's Do It Again *148*

r. A. bentinck

Sleepless *149*
Nightly Pleasures *150*
I Need More *151*
The Spot *153*
The Text Message *154*
Scream My Name *155*
Flavours *156*
Intimidation *157*
Burn Baby *158*
Exploration *159*
Catch the Fire *160*
Gradually *161*
I Can't Explain *162*
The Phone Call *163*
The Taste of You *164*
Thirst *165*
Forbidden *166*
The Kitchen Counter *167*
Climaxing *169*
chapter two *171*
Bad Girl Stricken *173*
Hellfire and Holy Water (for Katarina) *175*
Marinated *177*
I Wanna Know *178*

The *Seductive* Collection

Seduced *179*
Tea Lights and Petals *180*
The Afterglow *181*
Night Kicks *182*
Cooling Relief *183*
Speckled Sky *184*
Contortions and Distortions *185*
Sounds of Heaven *186*
Sensations *187*
The Silence of the Night *188*
Bulging Desire *189*
Weak *190*
Her Hands *191*
Let's Make Music *192*
Midnight Pleas *194*
I Wish *195*
Poured Honey *196*
Heavenly *197*
Day's End *198*
Linger a Little Longer *199*
Hindsight *200*
Shower *202*
The Sheet's Secrets *203*
All my Tomorrows *205*

r. A. bentinck

The Way You Make Me Feel 206
Pillow Fight 209
Foggy Windows 211
Her Fragrance 212
Peekaboo 213
Seething Desires 215
Teased 216
Memories 217
I Wasn't the Only One 218
Undress 220
do you mind? 221
My Plea 222
Lipstick and Stilettoes 224
Old Love Song 225
Read My Mind 226
Stranded 228
Play Naughty for Me 229
Catch the Fire 230
Salacious Lace 231
Boiling Point 233
Begging 234
Her Spell 235
I'm After Adjectives 236
Lipstick Stains 238

The *Seductive* Collection

Sacred *239*
Slapped *241*
Cindy *242*
Over You *244*
Never Knew Feelings like This Before *246*
Heartbeat Knows *248*
Naughty Girl *250*
Secrets *251*
Stop Knocking *253*
Natural High *255*
Play That Sax for Me *256*
Foxy *258*
1, 2, 3 .... *259*
Explosive *261*
Expectations *262*
The Racial Divide *263*
Susceptible *265*
Street Meetings *267*
My First Heartbreak *268*
Dangerous Angel *269*
Wild Heartbeats *270*
Touch Me *271*
With You *272*
Soft Whispers *273*

r. A. bentinck

Unchain Me *274*
This Yellow Rose *276*
His Josephine *277*
Before You Leave *279*
Baby Lean on Me *280*
Awaken *282*
All My Tomorrows *283*
That Look *284*
The Water's Edge *285*
Divine *286*
Under the Tree *287*
Your Company *288*
Finding Ways *289*
The Taste of Love *290*
Gratitude *291*
Transgressing Eyes *292*
The First Time *293*
Don't *294*
Whispers *295*
Her Skirt *296*
Captivated *297*
Rampage *298*
The Question *299*
I Didn't Mean To *300*

The *Seductive* Collection

Wet Words 303
Sweet Talk You 305
Drenched 306
Sweet Whispers 307
Walking Away 308
The Pictures 309
Nibbling 310
The Kissing Recipe 311
Probing for Honey 312
Rainy 314
Oxygen 316
Parting 317
Heavenly Hands 318
Embrace 320
With Time 321
Get Use to This 322
Time 324
Fiery 325
The Ease in Her Tease 327
The Mysteries of You 328
Wondering 330
Inseparable 331
Morning Thoughts 332
Kissology (the anatomy of a kiss) 333

r. A. bentinck

Take Me There Again.. 335
Mornings of Memories.. 336
The Wind and Your Hair.. 337
The look of love... 339
Starvation.. 340
Forgive Me.. 341
Those Eyes 343
Let Go and Let it Be.. 344
Expressive Eyes... 345
My Secrets 346
Tonight... 347
Just Surrender... 348
Stay a Little Longer 349
This Moment.. 350
How I Want You... 351
Waking Up To You.. 352
Running Around 353
Right Now.. 354
Tomorrow 355
Heart on the Line 356
Fluids 357
Obedience... 358
The White T-shirt 360
Beautiful... 361

The *Seductive* Collection

Lost in the Moment 362
Do It Again 363
Afraid 365
Can't Get Enough 366
Forgetfulness 367
Playing with Her Fire 368
Take Off Her Clothes 369
Sensual Vibrations 370
She is the Reason 371
When I Say... 372
You're My Poetry 375
Connecting Spots 376
Daydreams 377
Is This Really You? 378
Just One Moment 379
Listen 380
Seducing You 381
The Taste of You 383
Smouldering 385
Stealing Breaths 386
It's You and Me Tonight 387
My Love 389
My Inspiration 390
Acoustic Love 392

r. A. bentinck

Sunrise *393*
Poolside Beauty *394*
Sweet Sensations *395*
Indescribable *396*
Sleepless *397*
Overthinking *398*
On the Cheek *399*
Hard to Get *400*
A Ballad for the Broken (to My Sisters with Love) *401*
Closer *404*
Don't Go *405*
A Little Longer *406*
Hush *408*
Cornered *410*
Remembering *411*
I Won't *412*
Not a Player *414*
Sitting and Watching (Egotistic) *415*
Oohs and Ahs *417*
Heartbeat *418*
On the Dance Floor *419*
A Sweet Discovery (for Neelam) *420*
The Passing Smile *422*
Caged Scream *423*

The *Seductive* Collection

Bliss *424*
Comfort Zone *425*
Connecting Dots *426*
Ember *427*
Embrace *428*
Sipping Her Lips *429*
Footprints *430*
Her Hands *431*
Her Memories *432*
Hostage *433*
How? *434*
Hummingbirds and Bees *435*
If I Follow *437*
Infliction *438*
No Comparison *439*
Paradoxical *440*
Fantasising *441*
Cravings *442*
Feast on Me *443*
Indecent Proposal *444*
Intentions *445*
Flirty *446*
Lights *447*
Reservation *448*

r. A. bentinck

Unplanned *449*
Woman Enough *450*
The Dirty Looks *451*
Playful Lips *452*
Wanting It All *453*
Playful Torture *454*
Beautiful *455*
Close to You *456*
Earth Angel *457*
The Reason *458*
After You *459*
In My Arms (T.L.C.) *460*
The Taste of Love *461*
Your Fire *462*
You Are the Reason *463*
There is a Reason *464*
When You Smile *465*
Dewdrops *466*
Watching *468*
Wordplay *469*
Seduction Knocked *470*
Pillow Talk *471*
You Are Too Close *472*
Under the Stars *473*

The *Seductive* Collection

Skin to Skin *474*
The Closer I Get *475*
Let Me *476*
In-between Time *477*
Desperation *478*
Overly Excited *479*
Reading Me *480*
About The Author *481*

r. A. bentinck

[signature] Bentinck
Thank You

The *Seductive* Collection

chapter one

The *Seductive* Collection

r. A. bentinck

The Breakfast Table

this breakfast table is
reserved for dining only!

it's always
meticulously designed
to please
and to satisfy
the eating experience.

but today,
we break all
the dining rules.

plates get tossed!
drinking glasses
get knocked over,
chairs get shoved aside,
the tablecloth gets
extremely wrinkled.

the table is shifting
in countless directions
and this once neat
and
organised surface
has become a battleground
for
bare-naked bodies
moving

The Seductive Collection

with the flow of
lust filled rhythms.

r. A. bentinck

Fine Wine

you are like aged
fine wine.

you should be
slowly sipped
and savoured
from
expensive crystal
by appreciating
and
deserved lips.

never gulped
by hungry and
unappreciative mouth.
your every
flavour
must be
savoured
by all the taste buds.

The *Seductive* Collection

Hypnotic Eyes

i lose my way
in your tender gaze
as your eyes
wrestle mine.

i get consumed
in the eternity
of your stare.

your eyes
tell
a thousand tales
of tenderness,
love,
lust,
longing,
and
insatiable desires.

i get hypnotised
by your sedating eyes
and
lost in the eternity
of your gaze.

r. A. bentinck

Intoxicated

i can taste the
salacious words
at the tips
of your succulent lips
and
i get intoxicated.

i embraced
your glistening body
and
your warm
slippery sweetness
make me drunk.

i can smell
the pure essence
of your natural fragrance
and
it makes me high.

Just One Thought

just the thought
of you
and the days seem
brighter.

just a fleeting thought
of you
and old familiar
music
seems refreshingly new.

just one thought
of you
changes everything.

r. A. bentinck

Kissing King

she draws me in with
lips that's
tender and succulent,
she keeps me glued
with the slow
flow of her
honey flavours.

her kissing is
celestial.

with every smack
of her lips
with every gentle kiss
she keeps me
wanting more
and
more
and
more.

she has
transformed me
into a kissing king.

The Seductive Collection

Lazy Days

we lazed like
exhausted animals
on the first days
of summer.

we laugh
at time
as it wanders by.

we stuffed
the cares of
the week in
the back of
our minds
while we laze
the day away.

r. A. bentinck

Like Fine Wine

after all this time
you have matured
like fine wine-
bottled goodness,
priceless,
elegant,
ageless,
with a love
that's savoury.

The Seductive Collection

Linger a Little Longer

on days like this
when you look
so fine, i am tempted to ask…
please,
linger a little longer.

you light up
the atmosphere
with glorious vibes
and
electrifying smile,
why wouldn't you
linger a little longer?

i can't face the thought that
you must go so soon,
so i'm building up the courage
to say, please,
linger a little longer.

it's not every day i get to
see you this way,
you ought to
linger a little longer.

i'm running out of reasons
to ask you to wait a while
so please,
just linger a little longer.

r. A. bentinck

Morning Wish

may your day
be as bright as
your sunrise smile.

your moments
as excited as
your eyes
when you the recall
pulsating moments
we shared.

this is my
morning wish
for you.

The Seductive Collection

Romancing the Wine

she moistened
the tips of her
rose pink lips
and
slowly closed
her eyes.

the words poured
from the depths
of her angelic soul.

with every word
she was brewing up
chilled heaven,
a wine frenzy.
she recollected
the memories
of soothing escapades.

without sipping
on a glass
she made me
crave the opportunity
to sit and
dine with her wine.

she is a wine connoisseur.

r. A. bentinck

Flaming Desires

i want to
seduce you
to the edge of
your
flaming desires
where
heart-pounding sensations
steal
your breath away.

The Seductive Collection

Smile

i see your face
with that
happy glow
and i can't help
but greet you
with a smile.

i embrace you
with a flood
of affection
and electricity
ignite our embrace
and can't help
but smile.

you whisper
sweet softness
in the halls of
my ear
the kind of words
that leaves me
helpless with
a smile.

in your presence
you give me
unlimited reasons
to do nothing
but smile.

r. A. bentinck

Smooth Jazz and Fine Wine

a skilfully played
tenor saxophone
lured your heightened senses
and speak to you
in sultry tones
that's only
understood by
a thirsty soul.

unspeakable bliss
slowly coerce you
to sip some more
of the liquid delight
and you tamely surrender
to the subtleties of
your chilled seducer.

the liquid lure
gently approaches
anxious lips
while
dim lights
take you
on a celestial journey
where the cares
of the day
just drift
like smoke in
gentle evening breeze.

The *Seductive* Collection

Sunday Mornings

the ease of the
morning breeze
greet us
and
gently fondle
our wayward desires.

the whistling birds
provide just enough
music to fertilise
the burgeoning emotions
that's germinating
in our overactive loins.

Sunday mornings
bring
fresh flowers,
renewed excitement,
keys to release
imprisoned longings,
and
unexpected
heart-pounding
discoveries.

r. A. bentinck

The Aftermath

pitch-black stillness
in a cosy bedroom.

the moon
sneak a peak
through the crease
in the heavy curtain.

its beamy eyes
show the glistening
glow of your satisfied body
which
lay listless
in the aftermath
of a battle with
racy emotions.

The *Seductive* Collection

The Little Things

it's the little things
i wanna do with you.

i wanna run
and bathe
in the rain
with you.

i wanna stay
up all night with you.

i wanna cook
nutritious meals for you.

it's the little things
i wanna do for you.

i wanna hand-picked
roses for you.

i wanna play
the fool
for you.

i wanna be
there for you.
i wanna do
all these little things
just for you.

The Moon Smiles

tonight,
the moon smiles
generously
just because of you.

the sea breeze
whispers tranquilising
words of comfort
and we snuggle.

your company
lights up the dim environment
like a thousand fireflies.

tonight,
the moon smiles
just to reveal
another dimension
of your loveliness,
another dimension
of your lovingness.

This World of Mine

i close
my eyes
and
in this world
of mine
you
fill it
with unspeakable
fondness.

r. A. bentinck

Time

i lay
in your arms
for a minute
and
i get lost in
the moment.

i open my eyes
and
the hours flashed by
during our moments of
sweetness.

time has no respect
for me
whenever i'm with you.

The Seductive Collection

We Make Music

every time
our hearts meet
there is a familiar rhythm
that beats deep within
and we get lost
in the dance of
enticing emotions.

it's just one
of the ways
we make music

we create
our own music
with body
heart and soul.

every time our hearts meet
there is a familiar rhythm
that beats deep within

and
we get lost
in the dance of
engaging emotions.
it's just one
of the many ways
we make music.

r. A. bentinck

Whispering Flowers

flowers whisper
a quieting
and
inviting lullaby
to the honey bees…

come,
drink of my unending
fondness.
come,
taste my
fluid essence.

Pillows and Sheets

with a coy smile
plastered on her face
she declared,

*you leave but your scent
lingers on my pillows and sheets.*

*i relive
every moment,
every emotion,
every sound,
like it's the real thing.*

*i know this might
sound eccentric,
but when you leave
i can still
feel you,
see you,
hear you,
taste you,
just from smelling
the enchanting fragrance
you leave on my pillows and sheets.*

r. A. bentinck

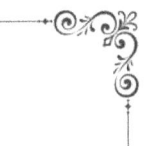

The Sweetness from Your Lips

i saw your lips
for the first times
and started
salivating over
it's perceived
sweetness
softness
succulence
and
sumptuousness.

the first time
we kissed
i tried to kiss
the honey
from your lips
and got addicted.
today,
i'm a happy lip addict
who has no problem
getting his daily fix
of kissing sweetness
from your lips.

The Seductive Collection

Naked

on those rare and
spontaneous occasions
when the carefree spirit
possess her,
she loves to amble
around the house
naked.

her every step
leaves a crumb trail of
temptation along the way.

she unconsciously toys
with my self-control switch.
her mindless saunters
trigger a spark of passion
that erupts beneath
my calm
and
composed demeanour.

a battle between
my senses ensue
each one fighting for
a position of dominance,
each
a victim of
her naked sex appeal.

r. A. bentinck

Cooling Relief

after prolonged exposure
to the
searing heat
of excitement,
we sought
cooling relief
by the only
available window.

fiery bodies
welcomed the
soft kisses
from
the cooling breeze
oh,
what sweet relief.

The Seductive Collection

Expectations

her relaxed body is
accompanied by
an anticipatory heartbeat.

her imagination takes
eagle's flight as
she waits.

expensive pearls
kiss her
priceless skin
that glistens in
the soft red light.

Victoria's secret
restrain the stirrings
in her overheating loins.
she is slowly boiling.

she is ravished
by delectable thoughts
and overcome by
the persistent
sensual anxiety.

she is trapped in
the arms of impending
carnal cravings.

r. A. bentinck

Making it Hard

i know
you can see it.

i can definitely
feel it!

with that
penetrating stare
from across the room,
you're making it
hard on me!

your electrifying smile
leave me helpless.

i am trying, but
i can't fight it,
you're making it
hard for me.

i am thinking of
all the things
i can do
to you,
all the things
i can do
with you.
you're making it
harder for me.

The Seductive Collection

i know,
you know
i am excited.
i'm trying hard
but
i can't fight it.

everything about you
make me
want you
so badly.
you're making it
hard for me.

r. A. bentinck

Curves

dainty curves
dominate the space
of the scented room.

every visual inch
of her elegant body
lures my parched
fleshly appetite.

her inviting smile
plead with my wild side
and
her innocent eyes
petition my carnal
desires to rise.

The Seductive Collection

Breezy Relief

simmering
in the afterglow
of erogenous passion.

we begged for cooling relief
in the absence
of a fan.

with opened windows
and
drawn curtains
we await the
lulling relief
of the
unpredictable wind.
we offer our bodies
to the mercies
of the sudden gush of
the refreshing breeze.

r. A. bentinck

Desirable

her silky voice
caress my auditory faculties
and
send shivers
through my senses.

her bright
and
inviting eyes
call out to my soul
bringing a fond smile
to my face.

heavenly scents
whisk me off to
a celestial place
where
she satisfies
my every fantasy.

In Your Eyes

that quiet look
in your eyes,
the one that
whips up storms
on the inside
sending my imagination
crazy.

that piercing look
in your eyes
that sends quivers
through my sensual faculties
leaving me with
uncontrollable urges.

that baby look in your eyes,
the one that
say more than
words allow
with it, i can sense
your unconditional love.

r. A. bentinck

Light Your Fire

i am always enthralled
by the thought of
enkindling your fire.

with just
one touch
your eyes begin
to glow,
your breasts
get perky with delight,
and
your lips
widen with expectations.

there is a fire
within you that
i love to ignite
just because it
heightens all
your senses
and
allow your desires
to burn
brightly.

The *Seductive* Collection

Signature Sounds

by now
my ears are
finely tuned
to those
familiar sounds.

those
prolong moans
confirm that i've
hit those erogenous zones.

those
satisfying groans
that speaks of
the bittersweet pain
you crave
again and again.
those
pillow muffling screams
that speaks
of your sweet release.

i'm always attentive
to your signature sounds
they speak of
your full contentment.

r. A. bentinck

Soaked

we are lost in
the deluge of
feverish frenzy.

our possessed bodies
become generators
of unimaginable heat.

a room starved
of fresh air,
the uncooperative breeze,
coupled with an insatiable yearning
trigger an overflow in
our perspiration glands.

now we are
tussling in liquid excess.
slippery bodies
glisten from excitement.

loud panting dominates
the ear waves
and
we toss like drifting wood
in rushing waters.

The *Seductive* Collection

The Shower

our overheated bodies
smiled at
the tranquillising effects
of the cooling
crystal drizzle from above.

water droplets
caress every inch
of her natural blessings
while
desiring eyes gazed
in amazement,
inextinguishable desires
fleetly
rises to the surface
once again,
suddenly,
clashing bodies cause
shower water
to splish-splash
all over the place
creating music with
a mouth-enticing rhythm.

r. A. bentinck

Unlocked

she sneaked
into the secret corners
of my heart
and unlocked
my hidden fantasies.

she nurtures
my wild sides
and
impregnate
the freak in me.

these days
my fantasies frolic
with unbridled freeness,
and
my imagination gets
tested consistently.

since she unlocked
my hidden fancies
life is more
excitingly carefree.

Against the Wall

pinned
against the wall
with limited space
to savour
her diverse flavours.

backed up against the wall
with no room
to groove and glide.

i'm relishing
the essence of your
manoeuvrability.

up against the wall
with little room
to play
we surrender to the power
of the moment.

r. A. bentinck

Late Night Dinner

with steamy lingerie
like that
let's do
late night dinner
under the stars,

where the still
of the night
sets the stage for
the soothing music of
the whispering wind.

i would love
to have
the pleasure of
dining with your smile
and enjoy the glow
of your excited eyes.

with erotic lingerie
like this
let's make plans
for a late-night dinner
under the watchful eyes
of winking stars.

The Seductive Collection

Her Pink Lingerie

erotic…
the first thought
that raced across
the halls of
my now aroused mind.
she painted
a stunning portrait
in her pink lingerie.

sultry…
was the image
she sculpted
posing in those
sexy pink lingerie.

irresistible…
was the smile
she flashed,
creating an
elegant snapshot
in her pink lingerie.

seductive…
the fragrance
she wore that lit up
the atmosphere
complementing
her spine-tingling
pink lingerie.

r. A. bentinck

Feline Tendencies

every time the
pressures
of
pleasure
gets
too much to handle
she develops
feline tendencies.

scratching
and
clawing,
making strange
and
indistinguishable sounds.

whenever
the pressures
of
rapture
get
too much to take,
anything and everything
is a fair game.

walls scream
from her clawing,
sheets wrinkle
under her

The *Seductive* Collection

vice-like grip
while feeling
the wrath of her nails.
when
the pressures
of delight
get
too much
for her to negotiate
she develops lots of
uncontrollable
feline tendencies.

r. A. bentinck

I Wanna

i wanna ride
you to the precipice
of your fluid imagination
where no rules exist.

i wanna flirt
with your obscene obsessions
playing your dangerous
love games.

i wanna wrestle
with your unending urges
just so you can
pin me into breathless submission.
i wanna bend
you like a bow
just to accommodate
my anxious arrow.

i wanna travel
with you to those
forbidden places
where we can live
dangerously
and
our hearts beat uncontrollably.

I Wish

i wish
i could extend
the hands of time.

i wish
i could recoup
those wasted years.

i will
do whatever it takes
to prolong
these moments
in
your presence.

r. A. bentinck

Impatient

hurry!
let's strip these
clothes off.
this changing process is taking
too long.

let's slip things
to the side
so we can appease
these dominating desires.

my craving for you
races ahead
of the undressing process.

let's skip
the prolong
foreplay formalities
and give in to these
overpowering overtures.

let's forget
the comfort of the bed
and take the cold floor.

hurry!
let's disrobe in a haste.

The Seductive Collection

In My Mind

in my mind
i can taste
the essence
of your invitational lips.

in my mind
i can feel the warmth
of your enticing embrace
which quenches
my insatiable thirst.

in my mind
i can feel
electrifying sensations
seeping through my bone
making me excited.
in my mind
i can do
all the things
i want to do
to you
just because its
in my mind.

r. A. bentinck

Peaceful Sleep

cradled
in the warmth
of her nakedness.
i drift away
in the bosom of
peaceful sleep.

her comforting caress
shield me from
the cold
and
unfriendly breeze
while i drift away
in a peaceful sleep.

The *Seductive* Collection

Pulsating Petals

touched
with tantalising care.

seasoned
to sensual satisfaction.

fondled into a fit of frenzy.

toyed
into heightened tensions.

i have given
her flower
full attention,
now her petals
are pulsating with gladness.

r. A. bentinck

Salty Nectar

in the heat
of the moment
i crave your tenderness.

i suckle on
your skin and
i can taste your
salty nectar in
endless abundance.

in the heat
of the moment
your silky skin
get inundated with
a brackish nectar.

in the heat
of the moment
even your briny flavours
taste sweet.

The *Seductive* Collection

She Said…

she messaged him
saying…
loving you more today
than yesterday
and
i know you'll give me
another reason today
to love you more
tomorrow.

little did she know
she just gave him
another reason
to love her
even more.

r. A. bentinck

Slow and Easy

i wanna sync
with your every
motion.

i wanna take it
slow and easy
savouring every aspect
of your sexuality.

i wanna hear
each heartbeat,
each accelerated breath,
each satisfactory moan.

i wanna feel
each slippery surface,
each tight grip.

i wanna sync
with your every
emotion.

i wanna take it
slow and easy
tasting every aspect
of your sexual magnificence.

The *Seductive* Collection

Suddenly

suddenly,
i felt
erected nipples
kissing my naked back
and i froze with
an abrupt erection.

suddenly,
she nibbled on
my earlobe
as if it were chocolate
and i understood
her endearing intentions.

her fingers
roamed the pasture of
my maleness
while her persuasive lips
glide by erogenous zones
at a slow
and calculated pace.

suddenly,
she spun me around
and
subdued me
with a deep
tranquilising kiss.

r. A. bentinck

Fantasies

may i
fulfil
the prescriptions
to your ailing desires?

may i
resuscitate
your dying fantasies?

mat i
breathing
new life
of excitement
into your reality?

The Seductive Collection

What You Gonna Do?

she stared
deep into my
vulnerabilities then ask,

"what you going to do
with me?"

with a tremulous smile
i replied

"i have a list of a thousand things
am going to do to you!"

she blushed as she strolled
by me with
the wickedest of smiles
engulfing
her delectable face.

r. A. bentinck

Whatever

however you want it
i will give it to you.
whatever it takes
to please you
i will do it to you.

i see your desires
burning brightly in
your eyes,
so whatever it
take
to satiate
those lustful cravings
i will do it
for you.

i can feel the claws
of your yearnings
devouring my flesh
and
i feel your breath
of desire
enflaming my skin.

whatever it takes
to quench your
blazing needs
i will do it
to you.

The Seductive Collection

i can hear
your heartbeat
drumming
with excitement.
tonight,
i will make music
with you.

whatever it takes
to make you sing lustily
i will do it
with you.

r. A. bentinck

Misinterpretation

don't be fooled
by my quiet
unassuming exterior
there is a sultry fire
blazing in the depths
of my sensual soul.

i have in my possession
the necessary
intellectual and physical
instruments
to break
your house down,
to increase
your screaming decibels,
to stimulate
your fluid flow,
and make you
weak in the knees.

i can nurture
the petals of your rose,
and activate
the curling of your toes.

The *Seductive* Collection

Don't Speak

shhhh…
don't speak.
we need no words
at this juncture.

you don't need
to remind me
of your love

i can feel it
in every beat of
your heart.

shhhh…
don't say
another word
i can feel
your need for me
in your comforting
embrace.

shhhh…
don't speak
we need no words
at this moment.

r. A. bentinck

Your Embrace

you wrap me in
your comfy embrace
and
the lingering troubles
of my day slip
into oblivion.

you squeeze me
with your summery desires
and i can
feel your friendly fire.

you swaddle me
in caring arms
and i get lost
in your loving-kindness.

One More Time

i don't know
why you did
what you did
to me
but
do it to me
one more time.

i'm not sure
you know how
this makes me feel
so just
do it
one more time.

you have
unshackle my
unaddressed yearnings
please,
give it
to me
one more time.

r. A. bentinck

Just to Please

i'm slow
and
deliberate,
just to please
you.

my attention
to details
are to guarantee
your total satisfaction.

the dexterity
of my
tender-hearted touches
are done with
one objective in mind,
i want
to please you
totally.

The *Seductive* Collection

The Teasing Game

your flower
piqued my curiosity
and triggered
my quest
to study
her intricate details.

each
exploratory touch
revealed so much.

the stroking
of her stamen
yield a quivering
reaction accompanied
by a flood of fluid excitement
saturating the surface
of her petals.

your eyes locked
with mine
halfway through the exploration
and pleaded with me
to continue exploring.

r. A. bentinck

Unfulfilled Desires

it shows in your
expressive eyes
that speaks of insatiable thirst.

too long
in starvation,
trapped by wild
pesky desires.

you have become
skilled at masking
your chafe cravings.

pretend at your
 own peril.
how long
do you want to hide
the way you feel within?

i have
the remedy,
i have
the serum
to unleash and satiate
your unfulfilled lust.

The *Seductive* Collection

All Yours

turn on
the red light
and tell me
your surreptitious secrets.

slide out of
your silk dress
and tell me
your deepest
darkest desires.

baby, it's all yours,
this is your
satisfaction sanctuary
and i'm here
to please.
may i give it to you
all through the night…
baby,
i'm all yours.

r. A. bentinck

Finally

finally,
after aeons of running around
in my pipedreams
we collide.

finally,
after all those
moments of make belief
sensual heat,
we get the privilege
to burn in
each other's flame.

finally,
i get the opportunity
to succumb to
the power of
your delicious allurements.

finally,
i savour the experience
of all
your delectable flavours.

finally,
i can feel
the sweetness
of looking into
your sinless eyes.

The *Seductive* Collection

Those Moments

you know how
to manipulate
my breath,

you know how
to tease
the logical reasoning
out of me.

you know how
to drive me
insane
just enough to
keep me yearning
for more
and more
of you.

i sit here in
the company of those
ephemeral memories
and the vivid pictures
still, rob me of
logical thinking
and leave me senseless.

r. A. bentinck

Led

softly…
she held my hands and
took me to
the sponge cloud
and lay me gently
for a heavenly ride.

skilfully…
she gradually turned up
the heat,
bit by bit by bit
till i lose all
my senses and control.

tenderly…
she guided me
through rocky roads,
aided me through
bumps and grinds,
through all
the countless
ins and outs.

sweetly…
she kissed me back
to a relaxing
reality where
my heartbeat slowly
returned to normalcy.

The Seductive Collection

Roaming Tongue

aimlessly it seems
but
somehow she knows
how to find
those erogenous zones.

with skilled precision
and
subtle dexterity
she knows
how to please.

her controlled
and
varied pace
with just enough moisture
send a rush of
unexpected reactions:
toes curl,
fingers grab,
nails claw,
and
high pitch sounds
enliven the atmosphere.

she has a
masters in pleasing.

r. A. bentinck

She is Unbelievable

she takes me
to places that
seem surreal.

she makes love feels
crazy,
freeing,
adventurous
and
memorable.

she knows how to
leave a lingering smile
on my face
and
countless wow complements
on the tips of
my satisfied tongue.

The *Seductive* Collection

In the Rain

surprisingly it
approached with whipping
crystal missiles
exploding against
our parched skin,
everyone pelted for shelter
except for us.

she peered into my eyes
through the haze of
crystal pellets
and
the unspoken message
was clear,

we will continue strolling.
our fingers embraced,
while we disturb
puddles of water
making delightful splashes,
we skipped
like carefree children
at play-
all in the pouring rain.

it was one of those
spontaneous moments
where unknowingly
we grew

r. A. bentinck

closer and stronger,
the beauty of this
fugacious occasion
leave an indelible stain
we don't wish
to erase.

The *Seductive* Collection

The Artist at Work

she asserted.
*spread my legs
like your easel
and
paint me with
your sweetest phantasms.*

she pleaded…
*dip your brush
in my palette
and
mix my pigments
so my vivid colours
can burst on the
surface of
the naked canvas.*

she implored!
*baby, please
don't stop painting!
i adore
the rhythm of
your brush-strokes
and
the painterly effect
it leaves on my soul.*

r. A. bentinck

Undressing

the sound of her
tight fitted jeans
unzipping
awoke
my carnal senses.

each…
zip,
zip,
zip,
zipping sound
massaged
my sensuosity.

her glacial and studied
unbuttoning of
the sleek blouse
further
enflamed my already
hyped-up appetencies.

excited anticipation
embraced me as
i waited
uncomplainingly
for the conclusion.

The Seductive Collection

Turning Petals

i turned
the pages of
her rose
and
slowly
she began
to read me
her story.

line by line.

i strummed on
her sensitive cord
with
my favourite finger
and
she started
singing
sweet songs
of appreciation
to me.

r. A. bentinck

Rhythms

your
slow parting lips,
your
rhythmic hips,
your
exploring hands,
your
gripping fingers,
your
panting breath,
your
low whispers,
your
gleeful pleas
your
exploding fluids
you are
a symphony of sensuality.

The Seductive Collection

Waiting

deliberately,
i kept her waiting
and waiting.

repeatedly,
i took her to
the edge of ecstasy.

slowly,
i search to find
every erotic zone.

watchfully,
i observed her
every move
manipulating the intensity
of each aroused desire.

deliberately,
i kept her
waiting
and
waiting.
waiting for sweet release.

r. A. bentinck

Unfinished

we rolled
in
opposite directions…
panting,
gasping,
smiling,
laughing,
and caught in
the clutch of amazement.

we glanced
at each other
and i knew
we weren't finished.

gently you
took me and
led me to
the place
where extreme ecstasy
flowed abundantly.

The Seductive Collection

Poetess

i slid between
your rhythms and rhymes
just to find the
right lines.

i frolicked
with your onomatopoeia
just to hear
your pleasure sounds.

i danced with
your similes
just to find
their similarities.

i stayed in
your moments just to
record your words.

r. A. bentinck

Satisfaction

too satisfied
to be bothered
we lay in
the laziness
of the moment
taking in the
sounds and feelings
of the sensual afterglow.

In the Dark

pitch black
but bright with desires,
i fumbled to find
her essence.

she held
my stiffness
and
guided me to the door of
her luscious sweetness.

i couldn't contain
the explosive excitement
that lit up the darkness.

r. A. bentinck

Glistening

she had that
glistening look,
her pores opened
and oiled her
with delight.

she has
that satisfied look
in her eyes
and
a mile-wide smile
that spoke volumes.

she had that
glistening look
because
she was oiled
with
satisfaction.

The *Seductive* Collection

Chasing Flavours

irresistible
was
the best way
to describe her.

one taste of
her essence
left me
wanting
more and more
and
more.

soon i was caught up
in the chase-
chasing
after her flavours.
chasing
after her irresistibility.

r. A. bentinck

Doing Dishes

the slow process
of
lathering
and
rinsing,

the slippery
ease with
which she squeezes
the foam,

the sensual arch
in her back
and
the periodic
twitch of her hips
leave me senseless
in a neutral corner
of the kitchen.

The Seductive Collection

Her

touch her,
smell her,
love her,
tease her,
please her.

whisper
to her
words she longed
to hear.

hold her close
to the walls
of your heart
and make her
feel safe.

mesmerise her,
leave her
breathless,
leave her
wanting,
leave her
with wild desires.

find ways to satisfy her.

r. A. bentinck

One

one
   look
one
   touch
one
   word
one
   kiss
one
   embrace.
one
   whisper

one
started
the journey
on this
unspeakable
experience.

all it took was
one.

Picking Fruits

her tree is
laden…
all
her fruits are ripe.

i picked
her cherries
and
her leaves begin
to rustle,

i tasted
her mangoes
and
her trunk
begin to bend,

i suckle
on the juice
of her berries
and
she begins
to shake
uncontrollably.

r. A. bentinck

Secrets

i kissed her lips
and
her secrets
began to unfold.

she had
enough
fire inside to burn
the village down,

she had
so much
softness
even rose petals
got jealous,

she had
tenderness
to last
and
last and last.

she had
so much
frenzy
that
wild horses seemed tamed.

The Seductive Collection

Tell Me

don't wait
say it to me
now.

tell me
your deepest thirst.

tell me
about those
unspeakable urges.

say it
to me
in simple words.

tell me
how to
please you.
tell me
what
tease you,
tell me.

r. A. bentinck

You're

you're
my reoccurring
fantasy.

you're
that sweet
aftertaste
in my mouth
that increases
my yearnings.

you're
the heat
in my flames,

you're the slippery in my slide,
the joy
in my rides,

you're
the bend in my bow.

you're
the reason i smile
in places others can't see.

The *Seductive* Collection

The Proclamation

she proclaimed,

babe,
your tenderness
make me
extremely weak

and

your machismo
make me
wet and slippery.

r. A. bentinck

Instigating

something about her
instigated the fling.

was it
the lure of her legs?
or
was it
the tease in her tongue?

something
in her that
provoked this fling.

was it
her intellectual brilliance?
or
was it
her inviting countenance?

everything about her
instigated a fling.

Let Me

indulge me.

let me be
the flavours
you yearn for
when you get
those
irresistible cravings.

let me satisfy
your quenchless appetite.

encourage me.

let me be
the answers to
your complex questions
and
let me solve
your unsolved mysteries.

r. A. bentinck

Dangerous

our eyes greeted
and i froze in
a moment of impaired attraction.

no words
just that constant…
am undressing
you
with my eyes
kind of gaze

and

when she finally spoke
it was
her words
that stripped me.
made my knees
weak.
excited me.
teased me.

there is an inherent danger
in looking into
her eyes.

The Seductive Collection

Midnight

you are awake
in my mind
and prancing in style.

i'm grappling
with your pervasive
sexiness all over again.

it's midnight
and
i can't sleep,
there are too many
thoughts of you
battling to
seduce me.

r. A. bentinck

Touched

i fondled
her mind
and
her body
erupted in ablaze.

i stimulated
her curiosity
and
a kaleidoscope
of emotions
overflowed.

i listened
to her yearnings
and
she rewarded me
with a bouquet of ecstasy.

The Seductive Collection

Transgressing Eyes

she perused
my body
with fleshly intent,
taking in every conceivable inch
with starved eyes.

it felt like
she was deliberately
undressing me
in public.

she had
a concupiscence look
in her eyes
with a lavish smile
that made me
twitchy.
i felt antsy
but adventurous
at the possibilities
of what she would
do to me.

r. A. bentinck

In this Moment

in this moment
nothing else
will matter.

in that place
i promise to stay in the moment
with you.
taking in all of you,
feeling all of you,
appreciating
all you have to offer.

in this moment
the only thing
that matter is me
being here with you.

Tonight

i can sleep
with ease
you have
filled me up with
sufficient goodness.

your legs straddle me
delicately,
and
your reassuring arms
remind me of
how much you care.

tonight,
i can fall asleep
with a peace-filled mind
just because you are
here
next to me.

r. A. bentinck

Of all the Things

of all the smiles
i have seen
it's your smile
i want to continue
to brighten my life.

of all the things
i enjoy doing,
it's doing you
i love the most.

of all the sounds
i enjoy hearing
it's your sounds
of gratification
i want to listen to
more and more.

of all the arms
that has held me
close
it's your arms
i want to hold
the most.

The *Seductive* **Collection**

Velvet Screams

muffled yet audible,
she buried her head
in the bosom
of the fluffy pillow
when she couldn't take
the intense pressures
of pleasure
anymore.

her velvet screams
was music
worth hearing.
they seeped through
the fibers of the pillow
while she contorts
with euphoria.

r. A. bentinck

One Dance (Gingerbay Café)

in a dimly lit café
her natural beauty
illuminated the table.

soft red light gently caresses
her luscious features
as slow reggae jams
dominate the cosy space.

Beres Hammond was
at his vintage best,
so i asked her for one dance.

that night,
the DJ was indulging in musical sorcery-
with every selection,
we sink
deeper
and
deeper
and
deeper
in a sea of romantic fantasies.
her now warm body so soft
i can taste her silky smoothness,
her head upon my chest as the lyrics
take us away captives,
my lips refashioned
from whispering honeyed words,

The Seductive Collection

to playfully pecking her forehead
to lightly caressing
her irresistible lips.

we are now drifting in musical waves
where slow dancehall
bump and grind
evoke fast and choppy breaths.
sensual rhythms tie us up so close
that the tip of my nose
skim across her steaming body
the heat…
radiates the soothing fragrance
of her arresting perfume
i am anchored!

we are lost in this dancehall sea
and time no longer has meaning
as we sail on from one
musical selection to another,
riding the waves of a multitude of
lyrical passion.

r. A. bentinck

Falling Clothes

in the fervour
of the moment
her clothes
began to drop
like dried leaves
in the gentle wind.

they collapsed in
a crumpled heap
below her dainty feet.

she stood there
like an unfinished masterpiece
waiting for the master sculptor
to apply
his finishing touches.

The *Seductive* Collection

Don't Make Me Wait

it's a slow
and
immeasurable tease.

she knows how much
i want her
but she keeps me
waiting,
and
waiting,
and
waiting.

the burgeoning
ache of anticipation
coupled with
my loaded imagination
leave my heart
in a spin.
my palm is
sweaty
and now
i'm breathless.

r. A. bentinck

Fatal Whispers

her approach
was slow,
sleek
and calculating.

she leaned over
with a devilish ease
and whispered
in the halls of my eager ears…

i'm the temptation
you are too weak
to resist.

i'm the seductress
who will tame
your wildness.

i shuddered
from a mix of
momentary fear
and
adventurous excitement.

The *Seductive* Collection

Scented Trail

she left a scented trail
of perfumed seduction
that could be traced
to the bedroom.

led by my now
uncontrollable
bloodhound yearnings
i tracked
her temptation.

she was reclining
effortlessly with
a mischievous smile
glazed on her cute
babyface.

r. A. bentinck

The Wild Side

take my hands
let me walk you
to the wild side.

hold me close
when your heart
begin to race
with excitement.

follow my lead
while we explore
those unspoken fantasies.

grip me tighter
when the action
get too racy
for you to take.
sync with me
while we ride
through the torrid
patches of unending
desires.

hold my hands
while we walk
the wild side.

The Seductive Collection

Dirty Desires

the first time
we met,
she looked me
squarely in the eyes
then whispered fondly,
*i got the good stuff
you need.and
i know how to please.*

with a befuddled smile
i muttered,
i hear you cutie.

she got cosier
then she murmured,
*i'm not gonna
lie to you,
every time i see you
i have dirty thoughts
and…
every time
i think of you,
i have
dirty desires…
you know i'm
living alone right?
wouldn't you
come home with me?*

r. A. bentinck

Steamy

the echo of her
pleasurable moans
swiftly
fill the space of
the small room.

her screams of
gratification
bounces off the walls
with excitement.

the bearable heat
from her toned body
clouded the crystal
windowpane.
we are now drenched
in salty pearls
that drizzled down
our sweltering bodies.

The *Seductive* Collection

Unchained Desires

may i
take you to
sensual places
you have never
visited before?

may i
guide you to
the brink of
erotic explosions
where your senses
get wild?

may i
tease the triggers
that makes
your liquid excitement
overflow?

make i
unlock those
imprisoned desires
setting you afire
while i watch you
slow burn?

r. A. bentinck

Risqué Roulette

alternating
feathery touches by
trigger happy fingertips
leave us tense
with anticipation.

dirty words
aimed
at our wilting
self-control
and
bridled emotions.

eyes locked in
an unflinching
stare down while
begging lips quiver
from the stress of
persisting desires.

who will be
the first to give in?
who will be
the first to break?

The Seductive Collection

Pillow Fight

like puppies at play
we tussle with
each other and
the sheets get rumpled
in the intense battle.

armed with
fluffy pillows,
mouths full of
playful chatter,
and childlike enthusiasm
we wage war on each other.

amidst the prolonged
fun and romp
battle cries morphed
into escalating yearnings,
bulges and bumps
begin to show,
tired breath
now sound like the calls
of thirsty desires,
we took noticed
and calmly we surrendered
to the power of these
new urges
and melted into each
others sweetness.

r. A. bentinck

On the Phone

the world now
revolve around
the sound of
your voice and
a piece of technology.

i'm enthralled by
your soothing
yet tantalising tone.

you tell me about
your longings
and how the time
seem to be crawl like a snail.
you tell me about
your specific needs
and
adventurous wants.

my imagination takes flight
as i devise strategies
to satiate all
your risqué needs when
we get home.

The *Seductive* Collection

Waking Me Up

her legs straddled
me in a slow and
sensuous motion
and
the electric touch
of her finger
was enough to open
my eyes.

it's midnight
and her pesky needs
coaxed her into waking me up.

her purposeful hands
wended its way to my loin
and
sleep vanished at
the hands of her
sultry touches.

she woke me up
because she had
some unsatisfied
needs for me to please.

r. A. bentinck

I Love

i love the smell
of your hair
as i slide my fingers
through it.

i love the feel
of your skin
when i kiss
your forehead.

i love the sensation
of lying in your lap
while we relax
the moments away.

i love the look
in your eyes
when your lips
greet mine in
a welcoming kiss.

there is a lot
to love about you
but most of all
i love
the simple occasions
i share with you.

On Those Days

on those days
when i hear
your pacifying voice
on the phone,
if only
i could reach
through the technological
barrier and hold you
how different
our conversation would be?

on those days
when distance separates us,
if only
i could cast a spell
and change miles
into inches
how different
the experience would be?

some days i just
yearn to be
closer to you.

r. A. bentinck

Magical Fingers

they know how and where
to touch me,
your fingers
drive me
screaming crazy.
    you have magical fingers.

your fingers have
a mind of their own
they know
when
to tease me
and when
to please me.
    your fingers are magical.

Speechless

somewhere between your
breath-taking temptations
and
blinding beauty
i lose my ability
to speak.

somewhere
between you penetrating
my aroused senses
and rendering me dumbfounded,
you leave me
speechless
and
breathless.

r. A. bentinck

Lavish Longings

the pulsating temptations
was too cogent
to oppose.

the congested room
was too small
for our lavish longings.

but we both yielded,
relinquishing the will
to withhold and control
letting
our glutton lust
lead the way.

Morning Ride

waking up with
a morning thirst
for your sweetness.
reaching over
you interrupted me…

my morning breath!
what morning breath?

i can't smell or taste it,
all i can taste is
your succulent
and
delectable lips.
i love
your sounds of ecstasy
which drowns out
the calls of
morning birds
at joyful play.

what a way
to break the new day.

r. A. bentinck

Shower Exist

your freshly shaven legs
emerged from behind
water stained doors
and you call out softly…

baby,
pass my towel, please.

beads of water droplets
decorated the raised pores
on your water-drenched body.

you tossed back
freshly washed hair
and your sensuality meter
shot up to steamy readings.
the appetising fragrance
of your bath soap
lights up all my senses
and
your irresistible smile
just drives me wild.

The *Seductive* Collection

Come Back, Baby

i know you had to go
but my heartbeat
keep playing a tune
that calling,
calling
for you…

come back, baby.
i didn't get enough
of you,
i didn't get all the time
i needed with you,
come back, baby.

i know it was late
and we were encroaching
on danger time,
you had to leave
immediately.

but i'm still yearning
for you,
i'm still craving
second chances
of the moments we created,
i'm still salivating
from the memories
you left me.

r. A. bentinck

come back baby,
i didn't get
a satisfactory amount
of your sweetness,
i didn't get to savour
your delectable flavours.
baby,
please come back.

The Seductive Collection

Dreams

if my dreams
were real
i would be holding
you softly
while we watch
the waves kiss
the thirsty shore.

if dreams
were real
you would be lying
in my arms
while i stroke
your silky hair
and
listen to your stories.

if these dreams
were reality
i would have been
consumed by
your sweet fragrance
while we watch
the stars play in the sky.

r. A. bentinck

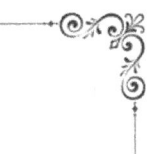

Take Back

please,
take back
all these steamy memories
and risqué dreams.

take back
the bouquet of fragrance
you left in the halls
of my nostrils.

take back
these sultry pictures
you painted on
my fertile mind.

please take back
all your fond memories,
my heart is flooded

you are absent but
your memories are
always present.

The *Seductive* **Collection**

Show Me the Way

there is no shame in asking.

show me the way
to your pleasure centres
where wild emotions
run free and they are
no limitations.

take my fingers and
guide them
to those areas that
make you tremble
with excitement.

show me the way
to the places
where you conceal
your unspoken longings.

just show me the way
and i will follow.

r. A. bentinck

Rainy Days

these are the days
when i find frivolous excuses
not to leave
the comfort
of our bed.

these are the days
when i rummage for reasons
to snuggle a little closer
just to absorb
your body heat.

these are the days
when laziness becomes
my close companion
and
getting out of bed becomes
a laborious chore.

these are the days
when holding you close
feels sweeter than sweet.

Whispers

bend down low
and whisper to me
those things you plan to
do to me
and
with me
when we are
finally alone.

come a little closer
and whisper in my ear
all the horny secrets
you wish no one
to hear.

bend down low
and
whisper those
sultry words
that make
my imagination
volatile.

bend down low
and
whisper to me
once more.

r. A. bentinck

Give Me a Reason

give me a reason
to sneak away from
work,
so i can fulfil
your insatiable needs.

please give me a reason
to drive for miles
just to be in
your presence
soaking up your sun.

give me another reason
to spend a little
more time
on the phone
just listening to
the luring in your voice.

just give me a reason
to find creative ways
pleasing
and
teasing you
to the pinnacle
of your daring desires.

The Seductive Collection

All Over Me

i sit in silence
and
your memories
begin to enfold me.

the feelings of
your soft kisses,
the roaming adventures
of your
magnetic fingers,

the essence of
your warm embrace,
the sound of
your alluring voice,
the smell of
your favourite perfume,
the angelic look
in your eyes
and
your ever-present smile.

i sit in contemplation
and
your memories are
all over me.

r. A. bentinck

Underneath the Sheets

she takes me to
fairytale destinations
whenever we are
underneath the sheets.

the warmth and comfort
of this fabric seclusion
is one of our favoured
places to be.

our imaginations are
set free whenever we are
underneath the sheets.

we relinquish the need
to be morally correct,
to worry about
the stresses of the day.
this is where we
make and break rules
willy-nilly.

underneath the sheets
is where we come
to quench our fiery desires.

The Seductive Collection

Drizzled Honey

in preparation for
the sensual feast
i drizzled honey
all over her already
delicious body.

each drip
and dribbled line
created
an enticing trail to
erogenous regions.

the slow pours
were both torture
and temptation.

tantalising
and teasing.

satisfying
and seductive.

i decorated her body
with
drizzled honey
just to heighten
the sweetness of
the moment.

r. A. bentinck

Reflection

i saw her reflection
in the mirror
from the deliberate
half-opened bedroom door.

the mirror smiled at
her nakedness
while she applied
sweet fragrance to
her delightful skin.

her mirror smiled.
the curtain danced,
and
i was frozen in admiration

of her reflection in the mirror.

The Seductive Collection

Fooling Around - Scene 1

she interrupted
my late night studying
with piercing nipples
like the tip of arrows
against my naked back.

she whispered softly
in my ear,
hey baby

then proceeded to
nibble on my earlobe.
my manhood began
to rebel in its confinement,
my logical voice
reminded me,

*you have an important
exam tomorrow, stay focus!*

ugh!
i hate it my logical voice
is always correct.

glancing over my shoulder
i watched her walk away
with a slow and deliberate tease.
damn… she is irresistibly gorgeous.

r. A. bentinck

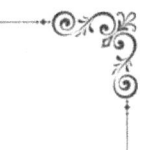

Fooling Around - Scene 2

i watched her prepare for work
and like a cat approaching
an unsuspecting rat
i pounced on her
with a gentle hug
and baby kissed
on her neck.

not now, i'm late for work baby!
she reminded me.

my intentions were crystal clear,
all the suggestive signs
were evident.
i toyed with her exposed
erogenous spots
while she fixes her makeup.
it was my day off
and my mischief meter was amped up.

come on sweetie, just
a little piece it won't take long,
please?
she wrestled my tenderness away.
no… you are going to
mess up my makeup
and you know what happened
the last time?

The *Seductive* Collection

Fooling Around - Scene 3

she stood in the doorway
dangling a Chiquita banana
in my visual field.

glancing over her shoulder
at me with a tantalising stare
she proceeded to peel it
slow and suggestively.

she flicked her flowing locks
aside while she gently
bite down on the soft meat.

with a desiring gaze,
an impish smile
and
a mischievous tone
she asked quietly,
would you like a piece hon?

r. A. bentinck

P.M. Scenes

the sun is at its peak.
and
an urgent need to
please and appease
raging libidos surfaced.

our synchronising hormones
were at their optimum,
so we initiated a
well-planned getaway
to satiate our mutual needs.

now we are
sprawled out with satisfaction.

our dishevelled hair,
the wrinkled,
disorganise and
liquid stained sheets
tell the whole story.

our skin glistened
from excess perspiration.

our languid bodies lay
stretched out in
a room filled with
the smell of satisfaction.

The *Seductive* Collection

Slow Surrender

it was never about
how
but,
when.

the process was long
and
tantalisingly excruciating.

her daily
drips
of temptation.

her deliberate tease
and tauntings.

the excessive flaunting
of her natural assets.

my increasingly feeble
willpower eventually
wilted.

i surrendered to
the callings of
her natural tormentors.

r. A. bentinck

Unbuttoning

my heart galloped
with anticipation.

the imagination is
riddled
with alluring imageries.

my loins ache
because of hyper contracting
muscles.

her unbuttoning
process
is slow
and
sleazy.
she is doing it
at this pace
just to torture
my will to wait.

The Seductive Collection

Pretty Feet

when her feet
hit the floor
even the boards
smile with appreciation.

her dainty toes
have a way of toying
with me.

she has pleasing feet.

i love to see
her bare feet
but they are even
lovelier in heels.
her feet appeals to me.

r. A. bentinck

Lustful Longing

as soon as i
opened the door
she arrested me!

pinned me
up against
the cold wall
and
unleashed her
raging desires
on me.

the buttons on
my brand-new shirt
flew like misguided missiles
everywhere.

Don't Stop

oh, baby,
please
don't stop now.

you've brought me
to a place
where i have never been
before and it feels
electrifying.

i'm feeling
feelings i've
seldom felt before.

don't stop baby,
it feels real good.
even though
am breathless
and
my face is contorted
with blissful agony
keep going.

don't stop!

r. A. bentinck

Penetration

it's the look in
your eyes
that pierces my core
making me want
you more.

it's the feeling i get
when you are
near me
that
question my ability
to please you.

it's the sound
of you soft breathe that
entice my imagination
and turns up the heat
in
my emotional thermostat.

it's the unassuming
things about you that
penetrates me
deeply.

The Seductive Collection

Let's Do It Again

what did you just do to me?
you have me
screaming my head off
in ecstasy.

you have
rearranged my senses,
you have
redefined my definition
of the expression,
'*blow my mind*'
and
you have me searching
for my next breath.

my squeals are
so loud that
we risk becoming
the neighbourhood noise nuisance.

i buried my head
in the pillow
to muffle the loudness
but even the pillow
fails to contain
these uncontrollable sounds.
what did you just do to me?
let's do it again!

r. A. bentinck

Sleepless

a flooded mind,
and an overactive imagination
laced with a plethora of
her enticing imagery.

my sleep is at the mercy of
her bodacious memories.

tired eyes,
an overactive mind,
nodding head,
but i wouldn't go to bed.

i want her now,
i want her
before i go to sleep.

The *Seductive* Collection

Nightly Pleasures

sweet seducing sounds
caressing my eardrum.

she is making music
with me.

stealthily,
her fingers glide across
miles of desires.

sexily,
she whispers words
that causes spontaneous eruptions
inside of me.
my baby knows how to
tease and please me.

r. A. bentinck

I Need More

leave your door unlocked,
turn off the lights and
light the scented candles.

pour two glasses
of your favourite wine.

i'm coming over for
more
and more
and more…
more of what you gave me
last night.

more of what left me
breathless and in a love stupor.
more of what cause me to be
wanting more
and more
and more
of you.

baby,
i am planning to make up
all the lost hours.

i need more
and more
and more

The Seductive Collection

more of what you give me
last night.
give me all of you,
i need more,
and more
and more,
more of what you
gave me last night.

r. A. bentinck

The Spot

after endless searches
he finally found
her arduous pleasure spot.

her eyes
glowed with delight,
her body buckles under
the pressure of excess pleasure

and

she whispered
sweetly
with a trembling voice,
don't stop baby,
please, don't stop.

The Seductive Collection

The Text Message

last night was magical!
your fingers were electric
and your tongue
was ineffable.

it seems like every part
of me you touched
just heightened
the pleasure experiences.

i love
your creativity
in the kitchen,
your explosiveness
in the bedroom
and your
tenderness in
the bathroom.

ooh, baby,
it still turns me on
just thinking about it.

r. A. bentinck

Scream My Name

i must be doing
something right,
we are both
sweaty and slippery
and
you are
screaming out
my name,
pleading with me for
more and more
of the same.

breathe baby, breathe.

i must be doing
something very right,
we are both
fiending for more
and more
of this breath-taking
experience.

The *Seductive* Collection

Flavours

i have tasted you.
now,
your irresistible flavours
are tattooed to my taste buds.

i have tasted those
gratifying flavours,
which are impossible
to forget.

they are plastered on
the decorated walls of
my prolific memory
and
they arbitrarily set
my body afire.

r. A. bentinck

Intimidation

she sized me up
from across the room.

she approached me
with confident strides,
stare me
dead in the eyes
then said bluntly,

i will do things
to you
and
with you
that you will
never ever forget.

The *Seductive* Collection

Burn Baby

here it is,
the precise moment
you have worked
diligently for.

the time is right,
this generous mood is idle.
ignite me.

poke your polished wood in
my unquenchable fire,
make me
burn.
burn, baby, burn.
watch me eagerly
while i blaze fiercely
out of control.

heed my passionate pleas
for more of
your fiery heat.

faithfully attend to my sparks
while they constantly fly
and add earnestly more wood
to my smouldering fire.
make me burn.
burn, baby, burn.

r. A. bentinck

Exploration

i lose myself
and
find myself
with you.

tonight,
we will carefully explore
all the available options.

let's
willingly unchain
our bridled passion,

let's
gently give in to
our feral desires,
let's intentionally lose
our restrained self-control
and
go with
the spontaneous flow.

Catch the Fire

you carefully lit me up
like a solitary candle
in the dark.

you politely ask for
more dazzling light
and
i burn brighter.

you ask for
more heat
and
my fierce flames
got hotter.

my wax melted rapidly
and i started
to worry about
my ability
to sustain
the consuming fire
you crave.

r. A. bentinck

Gradually

it was more
a slow burn
than
an engulfing flame.

her essence
and
her charm
took hold of me
s l o w l y.

she squeezed her way
into my daily thoughts
and
dominated my dreams.

The Seductive Collection

I Can't Explain

one look at her
and
suddenly my blood
start racing
through my veins
then
i lose self-control.

time after time
i try gallantly to figure out
what she has over me.

when thoughts of her
dominate my mind
my heartbeat
multiply times five.
i can't explain what
she has over me.
the thought and sight
of her make me weak.

my fierce resistance
rapidly fade
at the mention
of her name.

r. A. bentinck

The Phone Call

ring, ring, ring,

her: hey hon, how are you?

him: i'm fine and how
are you beautiful?

her: i could be better
if you were over here
and tear up all of
this goodness.

him: ha, ha, ha.

her: am very serious,
you need to be here baby,
i'm craving all of you.
him: give me a few minutes
i'll be there in a jiffy,
click.

The Taste of You

i have tasted you
now,
your irresistible flavours
are tattooed all over
my taste buds.

i have tasted
those gratifying flavours,
now they are
impossible to forget.

they are painted on
the walls of
my prolific memory
and
they randomly set

my body ablaze.

r. A. bentinck

Thirst

you poured
the opulence
of your essence
on my parched desires.

you opened
the floodgates
to my
starving lust
and
quenched
my
passionate longing
for sweet relief.

Forbidden

just because
they said
it shouldn't be done
we did it with gusto!

they said it was
too early to feel
this passionately
about each other
but we felt it anyway.

just because
it produced so much
exhilarating fun
we continue to
do it with pizzazz.

r. A. bentinck

The Kitchen Counter

this is where
the meat and fish
get chopped and seasoned.

this is where
the finer details
of the meal
get planned and prepared.

this is the heart
of the cooking activities.
but today,
the experience is different.

this is where
the love escapade is
laid out
and
played out.

this is where
bodies get
tossed and turned.

this is where
the bone merges
with the meat.

this is where

The Seductive Collection

the seasoning is
in the thinking
and
the cooking is
in the doing.
this is where
no salt is needed
to add flavour.

this is where
no sugar is added
to make it sweeter.

this is where
no pepper is needed
to make it hot.

just bodies
obeying the laws
of sensorial gratification.

r. A. bentinck

Climaxing

a slow
and
spine teasing
build-up.

a soft
and
sensual touch
transposed into
passionate
and
hair-raising
grabbing.

butterfly kisses
morph into steamy
tongue wrestling,
while our heartbeat
gallops like racehorses
frolicking in the fields.

The *Seductive* Collection

r. A. bentinck

chapter two

The Seductive Collection

r. A. bentinck

Bad Girl Stricken

i knew from the very start
you were never good for my
emotional health and stability.

but,
you had that
wicked combination of silky sensuality,
blended with a PhD in street seduction.

you drew me in slowly,
like a frog in the boiling pot.

i pride myself with being in control
of my emotional faculties,
but when you unleashed
your teasing repertoire
i became a docile lamb
excited about the slaughter.

the truth is, i was fighting
above my weight class,
i was fighting a battle
i never had a chance of winning.
still, i wouldn't surrender.

friends warned me,
mama counselled me.
none of it made sense to the
captured me.

The Seductive Collection

i followed your scented
temptation trail,
all the way to a place
where i lost my sensibility
and logical reasoning.

everyone saw my heightened
level of stupidity except me.
i was stricken,
and i didn't know it,
but my every action showed it.

one sip from your honey cup
and i was intoxicated,
i wanted to give you
everything i owned.
i wanted to sacrifice
everything just to have you.
i was an obedient pit bull on a
short leash.

i was playing a complex game
of sensual street chess,
and i didn't know the rules-
i was a lustful fool.

i was running a fast-paced race
i had no hopes of winning.
ever since she dropped
the one-night teaser on me
i was bad girl stricken,
and i assumed that
asking for more of her
was the ideal cure.

r. A. bentinck

Hellfire and Holy Water
(for Katarina)

she unlocks the fertile door
to your carnal imagination
and
throw away the key,
while taking control of your
now feeble mind.

"she is both hellfire
and
holy water,
and
the distinctive flavour
you taste
depends on how you
invariably treat her."

she is premium chocolate flavoured
glazed with rich caramel.
she beckons your eager eyes
to taste her intoxicating flavours
and
you meekly surrender
to your primal urges.

"she is both hellfire
and
holy water,

The Seductive Collection

and
the exotic flavour
you taste depends
on how you treat her."

her tantalising beauty
pins you against an
impenetrable wall of lustful desires,
while you grapple with your
social morality.
she makes all
the moral wrongs
seem right and
makes all the crooked straight.

"she is both hellfire
and
holy water,
and
the unique flavour
you taste depends
on how you typically treat her."

r. A. bentinck

Marinated

she took command of my
emotional strongholds
with fiery whispers
and
baby kisses.

her prolonged attention
to romantic explorations
marinated me
to the moral core of my
love bone.

she manoeuvred like
an experienced chef
flavouring
every possible inch
of my excited body
sending bolts
of sensual currents
lighting up all my senses.

I Wanna Know

i wanna know
what makes you
drenched with desire.

i wanna know
what spikes your
need to overindulge
in your deepest
unspoken fantasies.

i wanna know
what makes you
surrender to the mercies of your
persistent persisting
temptations.

i wanna know what
curl your toes?
what electrifies you?
what contorts your spine?
what fuels your
uncontrollable moaning?
what floods you with desires?
i wanna know.

r. A. bentinck

Seduced

i want
to seduce you
to the edge
of your
flaming desires
where
heart- pounding
sensations
steal
your breath away.

The *Seductive* Collection

Tea Lights and Petals

the door
finally opened…
tea lights
and
rose petals
illuminated
the faint path
that led to an empress
dressed as a temptress.

her aromatic fragrance
engaged my senses
and like an excited moth
to her intense flame
i followed
the petals and enchanting fragrance
all the way
into her waiting arms
and devoured
every bit of her
awaiting temptations.

r. A. bentinck

The Afterglow

precious pearls
of mutual satisfaction
dribbled
and
dripped
from her sensorial places.

her face glowed
with contentedness in
the darkness.

a sudden hush
descended on the once
noise filled the room,
we were experiencing
the afterglow
of an electrifying evening.

Night Kicks

pleasure notes
flowed abundantly
from the tips of her
baby soft lips.

her body wiggled
under the pressure
of overwhelming desires
and delightful sensations
while the sheet
on the once
well-kept bed
crumpled under the heat
and
excitement of restless bodies.

her favourite pillow
became the victim of
inadvertent kicks
and
fell to the ground unnoticed.

r. A. bentinck

Cooling Relief

after prolonged exposure
to the searing heat
of excitement,
we desperately sought
cooling relief
by the only
available window.

our fiery bodies
welcomed the
soft kisses
from the
cooling breeze.
oh,
what a sweet
and welcomed relief.

The *Seductive* **Collection**

Speckled Sky

the star-speckled sky
provided just
enough light
in a darkened room
to define
our now
glistening bodies.

the night was
silent enough to emphasize
the noises
of pleasurable satisfaction,
and with heightened senses
we could
touch and taste
the distilled essence
of this
majestic moment.

r. A. bentinck

Contortions and Distortions

her glossy back,
arched with sensual pleasure
as sultry sensations
penetrated
the essential core of her being.

her fascinating toes,
curled with
erotic excitement
as she tries valiantly
to wrestle the
generated electricity
from deep within.

her gentle voice,
dances in-between varying
tonal pitches.
her rosy face
contorts from
the ensuing pleasures.

her sleek body
became a glazed doughnut,
shiny and sweet.
she painted
a picturesque scene
of contortion and distortion.

Sounds of Heaven

she looks longingly at me
with the softness of fluffy clouds.

her innocent eyes
are illuminated window
to sensuous serenity.

when i gently touch
her with burning love,
she makes
celestial sounds.

i'm carried away
with her euphoric melodies,
trapped in her cocoon
of unending amorous bliss.

r. A. bentinck

Sensations

she is a
spine-tingling,
toe-curling,
mouth-watering,
imagination- exploding
promiscuous
kind of girl.

she leaves me
gasping
for elusive breath
in
the middle
of this sweltering day.

The Silence of the Night

come willingly with me…
let's penetrate
the peaceful silence
of the mild night.

let's give lavish credence
to our mischievous
desires
by intentionally setting
this luxurious room
afire!

come gaily with me…
let's strip
this glorious night
of its virginity
just to amply satisfy
our lascivious desires.
come eagerly with me…
let's intentionally break
the profound silence
of this sultry night
with the melodious
and distinctive sounds
of passionate lovers
at gratifying play.

r. A. bentinck

Bulging Desire

my bulging signs
of insatiable desires
snitched on
my secret intentions.

her glittering eyes fixated
in profound appreciation,
and her quivering lips
spoke clearly
of her silent consent.

we gravitated gradually
towards each other,
no spoken words.

eyes locked in intense
and unspeakable passion,
she consumed me
like a starved animal
at natures buffet table.

Weak

there is electricity
in every deft touch,
she paralyses
my senses
with her
sweltering embrace.

her every word
becomes an
unintentional command
and i was obedient.

there is something
in the divine essence
of her being
that renders me weak.

r. A. bentinck

Her Hands

she held my hands
and i felt complete.

the soft and gentleness
of her palm
said to me what
words could not say.

she held my hand
while we sauntered
in the pouring rain
and
the quintessence of
her tenderness
seeped into my pores
saying,
things will never be
the same after today.

The Seductive Collection

Let's Make Music

come...
come compose music
with me.

allow me to fiddle my way
around in the deep of the night
just to discover
the exact combination
of your musical keys.

let me tap
on your drums
with my stick,
extracting musical melodies
that fills
the still of the darkness,
causing the attentive stars
to dance in appreciation.
come...
come make music
with me.

can i place my lips
on the tips of your
saxophone just to hear
your melodies in amorous key?

come...
come play music

r. A. bentinck

with me.
come…
come sing
with me
while our deep breath
provides the perfect
instrumental accompaniment.

come…
come arrange music
with me.

come…
come let's get lost
in this music,
disturbing the peacefulness
of our neighbours night's sleep.

come…
come make music
with me.

The *Seductive* Collection

Midnight Pleas

wake up, baby.
can't you feel my need for you?
i know you endured
a long hard day
but these cravings for you
wouldn't go away.
they wouldn't let me sleep.

wake up, baby.
i know its past midnight
but i am losing this fight
i know you fed these cravings
multiple times for
the night, but they are asking for more.
more of what
you just gave me,
more of what
you just lay on me.

wake up, baby.
these yearnings are
driving me insane.
they are about to slay me.

baby, wake up please,
wake up, wake up,
wake up, baby!
please.
wake up, baby.

r. A. bentinck

I Wish

i wish i were
courageous enough
to declare to you
the carnal thoughts
i have about you.

i wish i were
crafty enough
to devise an elaborate scheme
to get to satisfy
all your lustful needs.

i wish i were
slick enough
to snatch you away
from the protecting arms
of the one who is
holding you now.

i wish i were
able to read correctly
your private thoughts
when you smile graciously
at me with desiring eyes.

Poured Honey

carefully i poured
some more honey
on her ineffable sweetness.

then i became
the silent observer
as it moved at glacial pace
down each
lush crease and
dangerous crevice.

i arrested
her rogue desires,
adding more wood
to the fire
of her already
burning places.

r. A. bentinck

Heavenly

today i got
the golden opportunity
to get close to her,
it was heavenly.

her pores radiated
celestial scents,
they were similar to
a thousand
sweet-smelling flowers
in the still of a
delightful evening,
the experience was blissful.

her charming smile was
generous,
her eyes bright
and her mellow vibes were
so soothing
it was truly a snippet of heaven.

today i was blessed
with a rare opportunity
to get close to her and
it was divine.

The *Seductive* Collection

Day's End

i wanna
lay my weary head
in your soft lap
and just relax.

i wanna
whisper the worries
of the long day away.

i wanna
lay awhile in your softness
and ease into the
bliss of the evening.

at day's end,
it feels great to come home
to all your loveliness.

r. A. bentinck

Linger a Little Longer

on days like this
when you look so fine,
i am tempted to ask,
please,
linger a little longer.

you light up the atmosphere
with glorious vibes
and your electrifying smile,
why wouldn't you
linger a little longer?

i can't face the thought that
you must go so soon,
so i'm building up the courage
to say, please,
linger a little longer.

it's not every day i get
to see you this way,
you ought to linger
a little longer.

i'm running out of reasons
to ask you to wait a while
so please,
just linger a little longer.

Hindsight

looking back over the
accumulated memories
trying to figure out
where did it go wrong
as the radio plays our
favourite song.

in hindsight,
i realised i let you go
too swiftly.

in hindsight,
i realised i waited
too long to reach out
to you.

i am sitting here
with your lovely memories
and my passionate heart
still yearns for you.

looking back over the
accumulated memories
i reminisce on the pleasant
smell of your flawless skin
and those silly grins.

you still ignite
my sensual senses.

r. A. bentinck

in hindsight,
i realised i let go
too hastily.
in hindsight,
i realised i waited
too long
to reach out to you.

The Seductive Collection

Shower

the water flowed
down her sensational body
from the showerhead
above.
its frigidness couldn't cool
her heated body.

glittering water droplets dance
to the harmonious rhythm
of her graceful curves
and
messes with my
stimulated senses.

she closed her eyes
in satisfaction and
surrender to the
delightful feelings
of the flowing shower.

the lathered foam
enjoy the ride
of their leisurely life
down her slippery and
enticing sensual definitions.

i am mesmerised
by the thought
of being in her shower.

r. A. bentinck

The Sheet's Secrets

if these sheets
had angelic eyes,
how would they see us?

would they
see us as actors
with contorted faces?

would they
see helpless carnal prisoners
or victims of blistering emotions?

if these sheets
could speak eloquently,
what would they say
to us,
or
about us?

would they
say we are creating
indescribable memories?
would these once neat sheets
spill our secret?

if these sheets
could feel
would they
scream out under

The Seductive Collection

our fierce and seductive intensity?
would the generated heat
from glistening bodies
tossing and turning burn?

would these sheets
be unintentionally hurt?

if these clean sheets were
neat freaks
would they fret and fuss
a lot,
over their now crumpled state,
created by our sensitive
insensitivities?

if these sheets
knew our names
would they call us out?
Saying adamantly:
slow down,
calm down,
just relax!

would these sheets
complain about being drenched?

r. A. bentinck

All my Tomorrows

she told him
for the first time
in their relationship,

"i love you."

he paused in the
luxurious comfort
of a satisfied smile
then asked,

"how much?"

she confidently responded,
"enough
to want you
in all my tomorrows"

The Seductive Collection

The Way You Make Me Feel

too often apart
it is ripping my heart.

hungry,
i prowl the streets
i'm in need of your touch;
your silly grins,
your pleasing face.

hungry, i prowl the streets
raging emotions wouldn't let me
skip a beat.
i am a caged lion
because you aren't around.

i roar for your gentle kisses
that means so much,
your succulent breast
i yearn to touch.

i roar in protest!
i want to slowly and
carefully explore your body,
every sensuous curve,
every enticing place.

i want to feel
your satisfaction flow.
i want to hear

r. A. bentinck

your divine ecstasy.
it satisfies me
to know you are genuinely
pleased.

i want to hear
your cheerful voice
and see your
girlish eyes ablaze.

i want to experience
the pleasurable excitement
of your body and
tickle the core of your femininity.

i roar!
too often apart,
it is messing with my heart.

hungry,
i prowl the streets,
baby, i need you!

i rage at society,
with its imprisoning concepts
i rage at the time,
it flies when we are together and
crawl when we are apart.

i rage fiercely at boundaries and fences,
we are so close yet so far.
too often apart
it is tearing my heart!
i savour your tongue;

The *Seductive* Collection

sweetness abounds,
your graceful lips,
those curvy hips.

i roar!
food does not satisfy me.
i am hungry for you.

i roar!
too often apart
it is hell on my heart.
hungry,
i keep roaming the streets
eagerly seeking
your scent,
your sensuality,
your smile,
your foolish grins
and silly expressions.

the comfort of your lips
and the calming harbour
of your gentle embrace.

r. A. bentinck

Pillow Fight

frolicking like
school children at play.
the bedroom has become
a romantic war zone.

pillows become
clubs and missiles,
and the mattress is one
vast battlefield.

tossing and turning,
teasing and giggling,
tumbling and ramping,
playful enemies in a mutual territory.

then suddenly,
one loving gaze
transformed the game.

all the fun and play influenced
both parties to meekly surrender
to the romantic urges.

at the end
of this new battle
two listless bodies lay sprawled
across rumpled sheets
in an untidy room.
too tired to move

The Seductive Collection

after a raunchy
emotional engagement.
we both gaze speechlessly
at the ceiling,
pausing to recover
and cool off from the heat
of the intense battle.

r. A. bentinck

Foggy Windows

the cramped room
boiled over from their
passionate body heat.

familiar sounds of ecstasy
filled the confined space
and it ricochets
off the stylishly
painted walls.

they are consumed
in an ideal world,
they carefully created.

the room shake
and
the clear glass windowpanes
get clouded with
sensual water vapours.

the fogged windows
told part of the steamy story
but
the sweaty palm and fingerprints
revealed it all.

The Seductive Collection

Her Fragrance

the gushing wind
brought a potpourri
of her enticing fragrance
through the open window.

my desires
get activated
and i start to slowly
download
her delicious memories
bit by bit
by bit.

r. A. bentinck

Peekaboo

she loves to play
peekaboo
with my carnal emotions.

she flashes that
magical smile
and my heart erupts
in confusion.

she plays naked games
by her open windows.

she sends me love notes
and explicit pictures.

still, she doesn't want
to be my girl.
she ensnares me with her
game of peekaboo
and i sympathise
with my anticipatory heart.

she deliberately
walks close by me
long enough
to torment me
with the scent of her
enticing perfume.
it's another one of her

The *Seductive* Collection

peekaboo games.
she calls my name
with the sweetest of melodies
and take time to be
in my company long enough
to intensify her tease.
she knows how
to peekaboo torment me.

she loves to play
peekaboo with my emotions.

she walks me to her door
but holds onto the key.

she asks me if i like strawberries
but have them delivered to me.
she is toying with my weakness
by playing those well planned
peekaboo games
daily.

r. A. bentinck

Seething Desires

she seized
my explicit intentions
instantaneously
and humbly i offered
reduced resistance.

she sets fire to my
overactive thoughts
which cause a profusion
of seething desires.

her fierce love games
sets fire to my loins.

The Seductive Collection

Teased

"you can't handle all of this goodness."
was her familiar and
repeated saying.
somehow it thrilled me
in a teasing way.
she captured
my daily attention
and my planning inventions;
"i'm gonna get her one day!"
was my quiet
motivational affirmation.

my curiosity give birth
to numerous questions:
how do I get cupid's arrow
to strike at the core of her heart?
how do I penetrate
her steely exterior to get
to the heart of her sweetness?
what are her sacred thoughts?

i sorted after
the wise counsel of elders,
and sat in the company
of seasoned love veterans.
i formulated a strategic plan,
with the sole objective
of finding a stealth way
straight to her elusive heart.

r. A. bentinck

Memories

i see the image
of your smiling face
in the slide shows
of my mind and all i can do
is smile and feel
truly warm inside.

i can hear
the reverberations of
your tantalising laughter
in the back of my mind
and i sail away
in the soothing
comfort that
fills my being.

in a strange and
reassuring way
you leave me
with so much
delightful memories.

The *Seductive* Collection

I Wasn't the Only One

i was sitting
high and mighty
with my bloated ego.

she embraced me and
told me how much
she cared for me.

but i wasn't the only one.

she tranquillized me
with her lady magic,
she made me feel
like her king
and
sang tender love songs
to me .
but i wasn't the only one.

she loves to play
her favourite
tunes that puts me
in the mood
then nourishes me
with her delicious food.

but i wasn't the only one.

she lit a fire in my heart

r. A. bentinck

and ignited my loins,
she fed me from a teacup
and fulfilled my lust.
but i wasn't the only one.

she guided me
to her secret places
and coaxed my racy heart
during uncontrollable moments.

but i wasn't the only one.

she made me to believed
she was my queen, but
i wasn't the only one.

The Seductive Collection

Undress

i am stimulated by your
potent words.
do you mind if i
undress your thoughts?

i want to get to the
core of your intellectualism,
i want to explore
your hidden fantasies.

i am turned on by your
uplifting words,
do you mind if i
undress your thoughts?

i want to examine
the source of your
inspiration and fascination.

i want to lie in
the company of your
dazzling brilliance,
do you mind if
i undress your creative thoughts?

woman,
you have got to believe me,
it's your priceless words
that inspired me the most.

r. A. bentinck

do you mind?

is it ok with you?
do you mind if
i undress your thoughts?
i want to observe what's
hidden behind
your intellectuality.

The Seductive Collection

My Plea

i am trying baby,
but am tired of fighting
these surging urges.

i can't conceal them anymore,
i don't want to fight any longer.

you set me afire,
you ignite the fuel
in depths of my soul.

it's the effortless ease
in which you carry
your essential blessings.

it's the electricity
in your inviting eyes.
it's the trailing scent of your
hypnotising perfume.

it's your charming and
friendly personality.
it's your sensuous simplicity.
baby, please.

i am counting my lucky stars
and consulting Shamans,
hoping i have
a fighting chance.

r. A. bentinck

my wilting willpower
has grown weary,
and my reliable resistance
is getting weaker.

i am tired baby,
have mercy on me.
baby, please,
i am weak.

The *Seductive* Collection

Lipstick and Stilettoes

her passionate words dripped
like warm honey
from those cherry lips.

they were the perfect entrapment
for the uninitiated.

her graceful strides
decorated the bland pavement
and she leaves
a perfumed beauty trail
you are compelled to follow.

the teasing click
of her stiletto heels
was melodic music
to the willing ear of lustful youths.

we were all innocent victims
of her pied piper charm.
we got lost in
the passionate following,
losing bits of our
moral senses daily
to her irresistible charm.
losing sight of our
sensible goals
just to wish upon
her sultry stars.

r. A. bentinck

Old Love Song

you are like an
old familiar love song,
you keep getting
better with age.

you sound sweeter
by the hours
and sweeter still
by the days.

you still know how
to make me smile.

you still know how
to make me cry.

you still know how
to make me feel shy.

you are my favourite
old love song. you get
better and better
with each passing year.

The Seductive Collection

Read My Mind

you really want know
what am I thinking?
come read to my mind
it's all there.

i know you know
you know my secret thoughts
i can see it in your eyes,
i can tell from your coy smile.

come closer, closer,
a little closer.

there is a riot going on
in my mind
all because of the way
you are staring at me.
don't play with me!
you know what am
thinking and feeling.

stop gaming me!
your eyes are undressing me
in broad daylight and
you still want
know what's on my mind?

i know your concealed thoughts
i can read it in your eyes

r. A. bentinck

i can feel it in your smile.
Come closer, closer,
a little more.
there is a riot going on
in my mind
all because of the way
you are looking at me.

The *Seductive* **Collection**

Stranded

i am hooked on her
glorious goodness.
i had too much
of her delightful stuff and
i am now wrecked on her island.

someone save me, please.

i am stranded on her
sultry shore
and the wave keeps receding
i am starting to give up hope.
is there another life beyond her?

there is sand in my knickers
and salt water in my lungs.
her hair is wrapped
around my neck and
her alluring beauty clogs
my judgement.

i am trapped in
her irresistible immorality.
too caught up in
her enchanted badness.
i can't get out.
somebody, anybody,
please help me.

r. A. bentinck

Play Naughty for Me

the stage is clear,
the audience has left,
it's just you and me
baby.
play naughty for me.

lay your lines on me
let your imagination
run wild and free
let your erotic
fantasies explode
on me.

lights, camera, action!
take one, take two,
take three.
take all the time you need.

just play naughty for me.
the curtains is closed,
put on your best backstage show.
just do it for me,
baby.

take one,
take two,
take three.
take all the time you need.
just play naughty for me.

The *Seductive* Collection

Catch the Fire

it was the brightness of your
dazzling flames
that beckoned me near.
it was the fierce heat from your
glowing fire
that lit my eager desires.

now i am surrounded
by your heat
and i don't want to leave.
i know i am playing
with fire and eventually
i will get burn,
but with fierce flames like yours
i will take my chances.

your glow caught
my attention but,
now i am here,
it's your sultry heat that
keep me yearning
for more of your comforting warmth.

the closer i get
the brighter you burn.
the more you burn
the more i yearn for you.
it's a wicked and dangerous game
playing with your flames.

r. A. bentinck

Salacious Lace

sufficient is shown
to blow your mind,
enough is concealed
to rearrange your
innocent imagination.

when you see her
you are tempted to cast
your judgemental stone.

but she waters your mouth
with enough temptation
to distort your moral goodness.

she is clad in
a bodied fitted lace dress,
and her perfect curves have
changed the nature
of this innocent fabric.

she has taken fashion and
turned it into something
sensationally dangerous.
she has turned
the street into a danger zone.
i see countless drivers
with distracted, roaming eyes
and unfocused minds.
she is clad in a bodied fitted

The *Seductive* Collection

lace dress, and her perfect curves
have change the nature
of this fetching fabric.
she has taken fashion and
turned it into something
salaciously perilous.

r. A. bentinck

Boiling Point

i am the water
in her percolator,
when she turns me on
and
the heat gets too much
i begin to boil.

when the heat is more than i can bear
i begin to spew steam
and make pressure releasing sounds.

i am the water
in her percolator,
when she turns me on and
the heat gets too much
i begin to boil.
today, she turned me on and
forgot to unplug me,
now am spewing excess steam.

The Seductive Collection

Begging

i don't want you
to leave tonight.
there is no need to go baby,
please, close the door.

there is so much more
we have to do,
there so much more
i want to say to you.

i don't want you to leave
tonight.
i don't need you to leave
tonight.

i want to feel your heartbeat,
i want to share in
your love songs,
i want to hear
your love calls.

i have a lot of stored emotions
to share with you.
i would give anything
to make you stay.
don't leave tonight,
baby,
please don't go.

r. A. bentinck

Her Spell

i ran into her today
in the marketplace
and just one look
from her and my heart was
on the floor.

i am trying hard to
get over her
and move on
but her taunting memories
wouldn't let me go.

how did i get so weak?
why am i always speechless
in her presence?

will i ever be strong again?

in the dark of the night
her memories choke me,
and my sensual faculties
wouldn't obey me when i speak.

i am under her spell
and it feels like hell!

The Seductive Collection

I'm After Adjectives

i'm hunting for adjectives.
    she is…
deliciously dangerous.
    enough danger to fuel my adrenalin.

i'm searching for adjectives.
    she is…
tender temptation.
    with enough teasing to make you
weak at the knees.
    i lose all control and
simple surrender.

i'm digging for adjectives.
    she is…
lusciously lavish.
    she possesses perfect features in
perfect places.
    i am under tremendous stress.

i'm rummaging for adjectives.
    she is…
racy and romantic
    i'm under her bewitching spell.

i'm sorting through adjectives.
    she is…
succulently seductive
    and i'm a slave to her sweetness.

r. A. bentinck

i'm thinking about the idle adjectives
that will describe her perfectly
      she is…
infallible infatuation.
      and i'm an initiated inmate
      satisfied with my sentencing.

am searching for adjectives
but nothing seems adequate
to describe her
in all her glory.

The *Seductive* **Collection**

Lipstick Stains

her lipstick stains are
in my heart
and the permanent smell of
her perfume resides in my nostril.

she has clouded
my love vision
and every girl after her
is unfairly judged
by her high standards.

she left her chip
on my shoulders
and i can't seem
to get over her.
her lipstick stains are
in my heart
and the permanent smell of
her perfume resides in my nostril.

her soothing voice follows
my every thought,
her images are stapled to
the walls of my fragile heart.

her lipstick stains are
in my heart
and the permanent smell of
her perfume resides in my nostril.

r. A. bentinck

Sacred

i don't want to
be alone in a room
sitting next to you.

i don't think it's a good idea
for you to come closer either.

you make me uneasy.
you are an irresistible temptation.

you leave me breathless,
and make me helpless,
i am scared of you.

i have heard so many stories
about you and they scare me.
just the thought of
the things you could do to me
makes me quiver.

i don't want to be in a room
with you alone.
you make uneasy.
you are an
irresistible temptation,
you leave me breathless,
you make me helpless,
i am genuinely scared of you.
forgive me,

The Seductive Collection

it has nothing to do
with you, it's just the stories
about you that they told me.
it's messing with my head,
i am scared as hell.

i don't want to be
in this room all alone with you.

r. A. bentinck

Slapped

it was like a fairytale,
as we stroll by the riverside.
we found a perfect spot under a shady
mango tree to rest our weary feet.

the fresh smell of
ripe mangoes
and
singing birds
made the moment dreamy.
the breeze was cool but
my thoughts were steamy.

she looked at me with tender eyes
and it fuelled my courage.
our eyes entangled in
an innocent gaze
as i slowly eased towards
her sumptuous lips.

when i was almost at
pleasure's gate
suddenly…
she slapped me!

my desires fell to the ground.
she looked at with
steely eyes and said softly,
"you are moving too fast."

The *Seductive* Collection

Cindy

she was
a sensational subject
but our verbs never agreed.

she was
tall and gracefully elegant,
and walked like
a natural model
on the catwalk.

she made the cheap-looking
school uniform
looked expensive and
her effervescent personality
made us felt like
we all had a chance.
she was the apple of our
teenage eyes,
in the prime of our puberty.
we were all hyped up on hormones
and unrealistic female fantasies.

she wore a smile that
broke our hearts but
when she shared it with us,
we felt like kings.

she was a constant distraction in class
as our imaginations often wondered

r. A. bentinck

to dreamy places with her at the
center of it all.
Cindy wreaked havoc on
the fragile emotions of
all the teenage boys in her class.
she was so close
yet way out of our league.

The *Seductive* Collection

Over You

i told them,
i will get over you
boy, was i fooled.

now here i am in a
sultry sea of
your hurting memories.

your smiling face
i tried to erase
so many times
but it was all in vain.

i can't seem to find a way
to get over you.
i found a new girl that
loves me true,
she is so much better
than you,

i thought she would ease the pain
but, here i am
sitting in her sweetness,
but thinking about you.
i can't seem to find a way
to get over you.

i turn off my lights at night
and i can still see you

r. A. bentinck

in the dark,
i can still hear you soft whispers,
saying things
no one else ever says.
you still make my heart
skips a beat,
you still make my knees weak.

i can't seem to find a way
to get over you.
what spell did you cast on me?

what secret sugar
did you put in my tea?

what did you do to me?
i can't seem to find a way
to get over you.

The *Seductive* Collection

Never Knew Feelings like This Before

never knew feelings
like this before.

you are the sunlight through
my morning window.

you are the singing
birds outside my open door.

you are sunshine and rain,
my source of joy and pain.

never ever knew
a feeling like this before.
you are my cold glass
of water on a hot summer's day.

you are my hot cup of chocolate
on a cold winter's night.

i never knew feelings
like this before.
you make my love flow
like a river. i just cannot control
the way i feel about you.
i just cannot.
i never knew feelings
like this before.
your love comes with a recipe

r. A. bentinck

that charms me.
you are my soothing red light
on romantic nights.

you are the music that excites
my heart and stimulate
my dancing feet.

i never knew feelings
like this before
until I met you.

The Seductive Collection

Heartbeat Knows

my heartbeat knows
just how i feel about you.
my heartbeat knows
just how i feel
for you.

what is it about you?

is it the way
that you move which
touches me deeply?

is it the sound of your name
that drives my heart insane?

only my heartbeat knows
how you torture me with
every silky touch.

you make me feel
sooooo good inside and outside.

only my heartbeat knows
why the sight of your smile
makes me wild.

heart, heart,
heartbeat.
only my heartbeat knows how

r. A. bentinck

you always amaze me
with your clever love touches.
you leave me feeling
so satisfied inside.
only my heartbeat knows
how you set my mind
at ease yet imprison me
with insatiable desires.

The Seductive Collection

Naughty Girl

she makes every bad
feels so good.
this is what a naughty girl will do.
she will set your heart afire,
and watch you burn
with desires.
that's what this naughty girl will do.

she will manipulate
your emotions on a string just
for the world to see.

that's what this naughty girl will do.
she will take your heart
and shatter it into a thousand pieces,
it would hurt so badly,
yet she will make it feels so good.

that's what a naughty girl will do.
she will paint your blank canvas red
and give you hell,
but she makes it all feel oh so good.
that's what a naughty girl will do.

she will ignite the fire in your loins
and leave you to burn.
she will walk away and
leave you in flames.
that's what this naughty girl will do.

r. A. bentinck

Secrets

she read my mind
and unravelled all
my mysteries.

she encouraged me to
be spontaneous and
i poured my heart out
in her secret room.

i begged her,
baby, may I have your heart?
baby, may I touch your secret place?

in the heat of the moment
she encouraged me spilled
my deepest secrets.
i have never gotten this close
to her before.
after years of trying
i wanted to make it count.

she whispered in my ear,
"tell me more of your secrets."
i told her I want to make
music with her,
right here, right now.
she muttered,
"tell me how you want it."
i told her i wanted to read her heart,

The Seductive Collection

and frolic with her hair,
i wanted to get her in the mood,
i wanted to lay beside her.

i took a chance and laid
my vulnerable heart
on her cold table.

in the heat of the moment
i told her all my secrets.

she ebbed me on to the point of
no return. she started
to open her secret door,
she stared into my eyes
and watched me come alive.

then suddenly,
she stopped, closed her secret door,
got up and walked out,
leaving me there all alone,
suffocating under the
pressure of unfulfilled yearnings.

r. A. bentinck

Stop Knocking

if you are not serious,
don't knock on
the door of my heart.

if you want me to take
you seriously stop playing
those love games.

all you do is play
with my feelings.

stop!
stop knock,
knock,
knocking
on the door of my heart.
am here enjoying my company
then you come knocking.

i let my guard down,
unlocked my heart
then you run away.
i refuse to play your games.
stop!
stop knock,
knock,
knocking on the door of my heart.
so you are back again?
what do you want?

The Seductive Collection

what is your aim?
i am tired of your games.
stop!
stop knock,
knock,
knocking on the door of my heart.

every time you knock,
i can feel your fire.
and it lights up my desires,
then you run away.

i cannot take this
anymore.
stop knocking!

r. A. bentinck

Natural High

the smoke from her lit spliff
refused to leave the confines
of her opened mouth.

it lingered for eternity
at the tips of her
luscious and succulent lips.

she painted a relaxed picture
with her bikini-clad body.
she created a masterpiece
on a vegetation filled background.

my presence interrupted
her distance thoughts.
she greeted me with a soft and
welcoming smile
behind smoky eyes.

she made smoking
looked so sexy.

her physical gems
coupled with the dancing smoke
give me an instant high.

after a moment's silence
she enquired,
"you wanna share my spliff?"

The Seductive Collection

Play That Sax for Me

play that sax for me
once more.
as her fingers search for
the rhythm of my body.
Mr sax man,
play that sax for me
before she walks
through that door.

her soft whispers
rings a sweet melody in my ear.
Mr sax man,
play that tune
for my baby and me
once more.

fading candle lights
in the dark of night,
her natural aroma
captures me in a dreamland of
unspeakable fantasies.
Mr sax man,
play that smooth jazz
for me.

trapped feelings scream
inside of me.
help me set them free.
Mr sax man,

r. A. bentinck

play that tune for me
once more.
please,
Mr sax man,
play that sax
for me and my baby
once more.

The Seductive Collection

Foxy

a caramel toned goddess
spitting lyrics effortlessly,
mesmerising your senses.

she knows how to
hit you on the 'hot Spot'
with just the right
words and with just the right
moves. that's Foxy.

she is blessed in more ways
than one. she knows how to
rock it like a
'big bad mama'
and she has the moves
to prove it, she's Foxy.

she hip hop's her way
into your heart and mind.
her raunchiness toys
with your decency
while she promises you,
"i'll be good,".
that's just foxy.
she is a caramel toned goddess
blessed with hip hop
lyrical brilliance,
her name is Foxy.

r. A. bentinck

1, 2, 3

you send me back to the classroom.
i'm educated, yet foolish.
i can't read your signals
and am having trouble counting
my lucky stars.

you have me counting,
one, two, three and
slowly reciting my love A, B, Cs.

every day, i am trying to decipher
your secret code.

lots of complex equations
that's way above
my mathematical love skills.
i am lost.
you have me counting,
one, two, three and
slowly reciting my love A, B, Cs.

every day, i am trying to decipher
your impenetrable code.

i rushed to the library picking
the brains of the love scholars,
i nibble on the tip of my pencil
wishing that would make
comprehension easier.

The Seductive Collection

still, am back to where i started.
you have me counting,
one, two, three and
slowly reciting my love A, B, Cs.

every day, i am trying to decipher
your guarded code.

i am educated, yet foolish,
foolish to the signs of this love.
make it simple for me baby,
like, one, two, three,
and A, B, C.

r. A. bentinck

Explosive

on the mannequins those
outfits look so sexy,
but on your sleek physique
they become
explosive,
dangerous!

your natural curves
enhances each
design principle and
you transform the fabric into
a weapon of mass distraction.

your mannerisms make
the designer looks like
a genius with eyes for only you.
you make fashion a passion
and you wear your clothes
with such graceful ease.

Expectations

the fun is in the anticipation,
it thrills the imagination.

the joy is embedded in
built-up feelings,
everything seems possible.

time is the fuel and
absence is the match that
intensifies the need
and water the seed of hope.

the satisfaction comes from
at last, experiencing it all.

lost in a moment with you
and one goal on my mind,
fulfil all the desires that were
long in the making,
today i will make expectations
and anticipation count.

r. A. bentinck

The Racial Divide

secrecy.
that's the way
we were forced to love.

pent-up feelings from
years of silent admiration.
we love despite the difficulties.

Sneaky.
that's the skills we were
forced to master.

prying eyes and chatty mouths
made us skillful at
evading gossipers
and
rumour mongers.
stronger.
that's how our love grew.

we flourished in an
inglorious environment
with limited sunshine and
lots of moonlight.
we grew closer in more ways than one.

satisfied.
that's how we feel,
after all these years

The Seductive Collection

what didn't break us,
made us stronger,
we survived longer than
the naysayers predicted.

scintillating.
that's how we are today.
our love burns brighter and longer.
we outshine the midday sun
and rivals the full moon on the
darkest of nights.

this love is too bright
for the dimness of those who
sought to kill it.

what racial divide?
our love is survived!

r. A. bentinck

Susceptible

truly, i don't know
how to handle you.

i am susceptible…

your waistline whisper
haunting words and
my heart starts
to drum up
a palpitating rhythm.

i am susceptible…

your cocoa butter skin
sizzles in the midday sun
and i am brought to
my weakest knees.
i am susceptible…

my eyes lock with yours in an
intensive sultry battle and now
i'm in extreme trouble.

i am susceptible…

you speak the language of
my fantasies and
my mouth spring water
like a flowing stream.

The Seductive Collection

i am susceptible…
you embrace me gently
and
i make a quiet wish
to the love genie,
all i need is one wish.
grant me one wish!

i am susceptible…

susceptible to
all the things you do.

r. A. bentinck

Street Meetings

standing at the head of the street,
that's our favourite place to meet.

from a distance, i have the advantage
of soaking up all of her goodness.

you make a mess of my
mental strength. watching you approach
from a distance is like
watching a master painter at
work on his masterpiece.

even the birds sing along to the
music created by your
smooth steps, and
the evening breeze blows
a refreshing and cooling wind
that sync with the sway
of your flowing skirt.

here i am standing,
burning up in the furnace
you lit in my soul.
no two meetings are the same
i don't know if you plot it all the way,
but there is an intrigue
that is present in each of
our street meeting.

The Seductive Collection

My First Heartbreak

she was my teenage princess,
my fulfilled fantasy,
my early morning smiles
and my late afternoon laughter.

the dew on my rose petals
and the happy in my happiness.
then one day she decided to leave.

i was dumbfounded.

my athletic knees became weak,
my lips glued with shock,
my eyes dazed with confusion,
i beckon tears but they were
too macho to come forth.
i never saw this coming.
she was the source of my
multiplied joy,
the light in my dark moments,
she was my everything.

then she blindsided me
by suddenly leaving.
leaving me,
in the company
of my first heartbreak.

r. A. bentinck

Dangerous Angel

i lay prostrate
before her
overwhelming blessings.

i am breathless
and soaked with
satisfactory perspiration.

my pulse is racing
with extended excitement.

multiple insatiable desires
nibbling at my mind
saying,
get some more,
get some more.
she makes logical reasoning
complex to accomplish
when she exhibits all
her glorious goodies
for me to dine.

The *Seductive* Collection

Wild Heartbeats

backed up against
my bedroom wall
by wild thoughts of you.

my heartbeat gallops across
a field of insatiable urges.
i'm arrayed in
beads of perspiration
from ravishing thoughts of you.

my heartbeat bucks
out of control,
i'm panting for breath
and refreshing air.
i am straddled by
intense and immediate desires,
my mind is on fire

fantasizing about you.

r. A. bentinck

Touch Me

touch me,
like feathers
brushing against my cheek.

touch me,
so i can feel the electricity
flowing from your fingertips.

touch me,
like you did before,
touch me once more.

touch me,
so i can't help but beg for more.
touch me,
so the hair on
the back of my neck
goes crazy.

touch me,
with good intentions.
touch me,
with nefarious ambitions.
just touch me.

The *Seductive* Collection

With You

it's not that i smile,
but
it's the quality of my smiles.

it's not that i laugh,
but
it's the joy in my laughter.

it's not that we make love,
but
it's the quality
of the love we make.

it's not that i feel bliss,
but
it's the quality of the bliss i feel.
it's not that i feel at peace,
but
it's the quality of peace i feel.

with you, there is a heightened
feeling to everything we do
and experience.

r. A. bentinck

Soft Whispers

she speaks to me
like the flowers whispering
a soothing
lullaby
to the
honey bees.

come,
come have your fill of
my unending
sweetness.
drink to
your heart's content.

The *Seductive* **Collection**

Unchain Me

your harsh words
spoken in anger
has bruised my
frail heart.

my heart is now
a stranger to
new love.

no one seems
good enough,
no one has
enough 'it' appeal,
no one seems
to have the
power erase
the marks you left.
baby, please unchain me,
unchain my heart.

unchain
this lonely heart of mine
so i can find sweet love again.
friends ask me why?
why i'm giving you
so much control over my heart?

i'm still searching for the answer.
baby, please unchain me,

r. A. bentinck

unchain my heart,
i want to love again.
unchain
my tattered heart
so I can go on
living my life
without you.

The Seductive Collection

This Yellow Rose

this yellow rose,
in the hands of the
wrong gardener
she will be
brutalised
instead of
fertilised.

this yellow rose
is delicate yet
strong,
firm yet
supple.
her petals the
essence of
smooth sensuality.
this yellow rose,
in the eyes
of the right
admirer
will be idolise
rather than
demoralised.
this yellow rose
must be honoured
and treasured.

r. A. bentinck

His Josephine

when all his hopes
were diminished
there she was
with her ever glowing smile.

he was captured.

he didn't know how
to stop feeling
this way about her.

how should they explain
these feelings that
captured them by surprise?

how do they justify
the look in each
other's eyes?

they longed to
let go and
fall into each other
arms without fear.
what should they do?
should they break
all the rules?

they don't know
how to curb and

The Seductive Collection

harness their spontaneous feelings.
when they think about
each other
they can feel those
fresh feelings
that carries them away
to a place where there is
no inhibitions or fear.

r. A. bentinck

Before You Leave

before you leave
may i see you smile
one more time,
so i can capture and
bottle this moment?

before you leave
may i ask you to speak
once more,
so i can savour
the essence of your voice
until we meet again?

before you leave
may i look at you
one more time
to preserve this image
in the gallery of my mind?

before you leave
can you pass close by me
so i can savour
your compelling scent
the umpteenth time?

before you leave
may i have the privilege
of experiencing all of you?

The Seductive Collection

Baby Lean on Me

i may not have
the medication
to ease your sadness.

i may not have
the pill
to ease the pains
of your heartbreaks.

but i have
attentive ears
and
robust shoulders,

baby, you can lean on me.
i may not know the
beginnings and endings
of all your sad stories.

i might never comprehend
the feelings of the shattered memories
you fall asleep with
at nights. but,
you have my undivided attention
and good intentions,

baby, lean on me.
i see the pain in

r. A. bentinck

your glowing smile
and the dullness in
your shiny eyes.
i may not always understand,
but I can empathise.
when it all gets too much,
baby, just lean on me.

you can lean on me.

The *Seductive* Collection

Awaken

she stirred parts of him
that was fast asleep.

she knows how to
open the closed doors
to his tender heart.

she caused him
to bloom in a whole new way.

she strolled into
his life with sensual grace
and set his uneasy heart
at ease.

r. A. bentinck

All My Tomorrows

she told him
for the first time
in their relationship,

"i love you."

he paused in
the comfort of a smile
then asked,

"how much?"

she responded,
"enough
to want you in
all my tomorrows"

That Look

there is a certain look
in your eyes
when we exchange
a gentle glance.

that look
which speaks of
a profound appreciation
that words cannot explain.

that look you give
when the flood of pleasing emotions
gets the better of you.

that look which says,
the feeling is mutual,

that look that says
we don't need words,

that look which penetrates me
to the core of my being.

that look you so often give me.

r. A. bentinck

The Water's Edge

i love the way
the wind takes your hair
away in its gentle gush.

i cherish the way
our hands feel
entwined in the moment
while we stroll along
the water ways.

i value the ease
of our conversations
and i enjoy the way
the words slide off
the tip of your
delicious tongue.

i savour the way
the morning sun
wraps your body
with its golden drape.

The Seductive Collection

Divine

i just want to
let you know,
that
you're a blessing.

your smile is the
embodiment of
blissful peace.

you light up
my life with
your natural radiance.

you come bearing
gifts of perfumed
delight and hands full
of pleasant vibes.
you are more than
beautiful,
you are a divine gift.

r. A. bentinck

Under the Tree

the birds sing a
melodious song
that fills the afternoon atmosphere.

lying playfully
in my lap her
eyes tell a thousand tales
of comfort and peace.

we relax the hours
away while listening
to the twilight sounds
calling from a distance.
it's almost time to head home.

The Seductive Collection

Your Company

may i hold your soft hands?
i just want you
to know that
i really care.

may i wipe away your fears?
i just want
to be there
for you.

may i hold you close?
i just want to feel
the warmth of your embrace.

may i sit in your company?
i just want to
listen to your angelic voice
over and over again.

r. A. bentinck

Finding Ways

i will continue to
explore ways
to show you
how i feel about you.

i will continue to find
one hundred ways
to say to you
how much
i cherish you.

i will continue to
find ways and means
daily to show how much
i care about you.

The *Seductive* **Collection**

The Taste of Love

you are
what love taste like.
    you are
what love feels like.
    you are
what love smells like.
    you are
what love sounds like.

in so many unforgettable ways
you embody
the true essence of
a divine love.

r. A. bentinck

Gratitude

for the sense of sight,
i give thanks
just because
i can see you in
all your sensual glory.

for the sense of touch,
i give thanks
because i can feel
your silky smoothness
and i know its
more than luck.

for the sense of smell,
i give thanks
just because
i can smell your fragrances
that lights up my days.

for the sense of hearing,
i give thanks
because of your smooth voice
there is always a reason to smile.

The Seductive Collection

Transgressing Eyes

she perused
my body
with fleshly intent,
taking in every
conceivable inch
with starved eyes.

it felt like
she was deliberately
undressing me in public.

she had
a concupiscence look
in her eyes
with a lavish smile
that made me
twitchy.
i felt antsy
but adventurous at the possibilities
of what she could do to me.

r. A. bentinck

The First Time

the first time
i laid my palms
on her was to provide
a comforting massage.

my oil-filled hands
slide around each
wonderful arch,
each desirable bend
and seductive section.

the first time
my fingers kissed
her envious body
i learned the mysteries
to her irresistibility.

her flesh was
a gentle persuader and
i started to envisioned
the unlimited possibilities
of being with her.

The *Seductive* Collection

Don't

don't tease me
if you don't intend
to please me.

don't spark
my desires
unless you will
set them afire.

don't stimulate
my yearnings
unless you can
appease my
insatiable longings.

this is no game!
my feelings
and needs
i take seriously.

don't tease me
if you have no intentions
of pleasing me.
please, don't!

r. A. bentinck

Whispers

she gently
glide the tips of her nose
across the side of my face
and paused by my ear
to whisper
sweet obscenities
while her desiring breath
torches the core of my
sizzling needs.

i submitted to her
exorbitant requests.
she coaxed me
to gradually open up
and i became weak to her
tantalising touch.

The *Seductive* Collection

Her Skirt

her skirt,
long enough to
conceal her tease
and
short enough to
explode the ticking
imagination.

her skirt,
tight enough to
caress each sensual curve
and loose enough to
facilitate the strides
of her elegant legs.

r. A. bentinck

Captivated

she seized
my senses
and held me captive
with her facile charm.

her smile oozes
its way into the crevices
of my imagination
and
there it activated
all
my dormant longings.

The Seductive Collection

Rampage

after hours of
company meeting
and business formalities.
finally,
we are alone together.

we exhaled in unison.

she smiled at me
and my thoughts
set off on a rampage.

she held my hands
tenderly and blood begins
to flow to emergency places.

she moved in for an
affectionate embrace
and all sensuous hell
broke loose.

r. A. bentinck

The Question

what would it be like
to be with her?

i questioned myself
for the umpteen time.

immediately
my imagination
provided answers.
now,

i can see your
gentle hands roaming
my fields.

i can taste the lipstick
on your enticing lips,

i can feel your silken hair
sweep across my chest,

i can inhale the playful scent
of your Daisy perfume
by Marc Jacobs
and i am hooked on
your euphoria.

The Seductive Collection

I Didn't Mean To

i didn't mean
to fall for you
but i did.

i didn't know
that i would
want you so often
but i did.

i didn't know
you could love me
this much
but you did.

i didn't mean
to fall for you
but i am glad
i did.

r. A. bentinck

chapter three

The Seductive Collection

r. A. bentinck

Wet Words

there is something about
your endearing words
that makes me wet.

they turn me on like
a running pipe, and
get me so sexcited.

your poetic dexterity
leaves me weak
in the knees.

have me steaming up
in my clean clothes,
swiftly activating
the freak in me,

making my elegant dress
falls slowly
to the floor.

i get wild with excitement
at the thought of experiencing
the reality of your every word.

there is something about
those descriptive words of yours
that makes me wet.
something about your powerful

The Seductive Collection

imageries that ignite a fire
in this fertile mind,
your words turn me on
like a pipe.

what are you trying to do
to me?
can you fulfill
the promises in your every word?

can you satisfy my wild and freaky side?
can you tame these raging emotions
before it gets crazier in my mind?

r. A. bentinck

Sweet Talk You

may i have a moment
of your time?
i want to sweet talk you.
i want to tell you
about the joys you bring me.

may i speak to you
away from prying eyes?
i want to sweet talk you.
i want to tell you how much
you mean to me,

may i have a few minutes
of your precious time?
i want to sweet talk you.

i want to sit in
the company of
your radiant smile
and tell you stories while
i get lost in your angelic eyes.

may i have a moment
with you?
i just want
to sweet talk you.

The *Seductive* Collection

Drenched

i am drenched
with desires for you.
you showed me a snippet of
your sweetness and now
i'm left with uncontrollable longings.
i am drenched
with desires for you.

your irresistible blessings
keep toying with me,
you test my self-control
and logical reasoning daily
i am drenched
with desires about you.

i am drenched
with your tantalizing tendencies,
your butterfly gaze,
your sugary smile,
your graceful walk
and your tranquillizing voice.

i am drenched
with insatiable desires for you.

r. A. bentinck

Sweet Whispers

my lips to your ears
whispering the sweet secrets
you long to hear.

my lips to your ears
saying all the tasteful things
you want to hear.

my lips to your ear
whispering slowly
while i smell
the delightful fragrance
of your hair.

my lips to your ears
telling you
the pleasing things
just to light up your
bright and graceful smile.

The Seductive Collection

Walking Away

there is something
mesmerizing
about her
when she gracefully
walks away.

her tender feet
romance the pebbles
on
the dusty road,

her hip sways
to the gentle music of
the whispering wind,

and she leaves
a tantalising trail of her
enticing fragrance
along the way.

she makes me
want to ask her
to stay a little longer.

r. A. bentinck

The Pictures

she sent me her pictures
today
and my descriptive engines
got turned on:

she oozed sensuality
in endless ways,

she was a refreshing
breath arresting beauty,

she looked
stunningly gorgeous,

she was the delicious
candy of my eyes,
she was the heat
in my consuming flame,
she caused the lust
in my burgeoning desires,
and the icing
on my easy-going day.

she sent me her pictures
today and it was
the sweetest surprises
in so many ways.

The *Seductive* Collection

Nibbling

i nibbled on
her earlobes and
she erupted
with steamy passion.

i can feel her quivering body
begging for more,

i could see her body
contorts in the heat of
the moment's flame.

so i nibbled on
her earlobes some more
and her body
became overheated with
insatiable desires.
i deliberately nibbled on
her earlobes just
to stoke the fire of
her inner consuming lust.

i nibbled and
nibbled and nibbled
just to taste
her sweetness
with my lips,
and exploring tongue.

r. A. bentinck

The Kissing Recipe

- one ounce of
willingness,
- add tender touches to taste,
an unlimited amount of
lips and tongues.

- a dash a wild imagination
and a sprinkle of
lust filled desires.

- the soft closing of
the eyes are preferential.

- add a healthy dose
of tongue wrestling skills
and a small portion
of courage to be
fully involve in
the ensuing friendly battle.

mixed all ingredients
to personal taste
and satisfaction.

bon appétit.

The Seductive Collection

Probing for Honey

i was the persistent honeybee
who instinctively knew
what she was concealing
behind those tightly sealed lips.

so i probed and prod
with my exploring tongue.

i gentle kissed and smacked
her lips but
her steel barrier teeth
didn't make it easy for me.

so i invoked
my persuasive qualities.
i begged and i pleaded,
i coaxed and i cajoled,
i stayed patient and calm
throughout the initial ordeal.

her petal lips encouraged me
along the way,
her enticing fragrance
enflamed my senses
and kept me motivated.

then after countless
probes and prods
she relented.

r. A. bentinck

oh, the emotions that followed.
her honey aura was more
than i imagined,
her lips were softer than soft,
her tongue was simply magical,
and the sensation of it all
was euphoric.

she gives me a taste of
her honey flavours
and left me with
a sugary high.

The *Seductive* Collection

Rainy

it's raining
but that doesn't mean
a thing.

we will sit
right here and
get soaked.

soaked
by the raindrops,

soaked
by our drizzling passion,

drenched by
the deluge of irresistible desires.

it's raining.
so what?
we are not going anywhere.

we will stay right here
and get soaked in
the downpour of
this moment's emotions.

at the end
we will be wet,
but

r. A. bentinck

aroused to
the sweet taste of
our closeness,
aroused by
our body heat,
and
aroused by
our irresistible blessings.

The Seductive Collection

Oxygen

if it's not oxygen
why do i feel like
i'm going to die without it?

it's not like oxygen
but it feels like
i cannot survive without it.

if it's not oxygen
why i'm breathless
and suffocating?

it's not like oxygen
but i'm struggling
to breath without it.
i'm craving
your sweet lips against mine,
i'm craving
your warm and comforting caress.

it's not oxygen
but it seems like i need
your succulent kisses daily
just to stay alive.

r. A. bentinck

Parting

time invariably
finds a way to fly
when we are together.

time spent together is
delectable.
we are always too caught in
the moment's beauty
to see when time passes us by.

too wrapped up
in each other's presence
to pay attention to time.

until we meet again
i will hold your memories close,
i will cherish the moments shared,
i will savour
your every touch,
every embrace,
every word we shared.

our partings are always
bittersweet because
the flying time always
finds a way to leave us yearning
for more time to be together.

The Seductive Collection

Heavenly Hands

she willingly gave me her hands
today
and my whole world changed.

her hands felt like
the soft petals of a rose
and they smelled like perfume
from the sweetest of flowers.

she tenderly touched my cheek
today
and rearrange
my inner world.

her gentle hands were
my soft cloud,
my comforting pillow,
they were much more
than i imagined.

i gentle held her hands today
and my world will never
be the same again.

she offered me her hands
and they stole my heart away.

before today i never knew
holding someone's hands

r. A. bentinck

could be this breathtaking
but
when she gave me her hands
today
she opened up
a whole new world for me.

The Seductive Collection

Embrace

it felt so good
to finally feel
her body heat.

her warmth satiated me
on a cold evening.

the gentleness of
her touch sends
bolts of enticing electricity
seeping through my
excited body.

her magnetic fingers
slowly massage me
and a soothing and
desiring sensation
accompanied her every touch.

her breath of longing
caresses the raised pores
on my neck. and something
about this entire moment
makes me weak to
all of her sweetness.

r. A. bentinck

With Time

given time
i have gradually come
to realise the inherent sweetness
that lies beneath
her masked exterior.

she knows how
to delight and tease me.
she knows how
to flirt skillfully
with juicy words
that toy with me
in strategic places.

she knows when
to flash that alluring smile
while glancing slyly at me
with gentle eyes
that strip away all
my formidable defenses
and my sense of
moral rightness.

given time she has grown on me,
she mesmerizes me,
she entices me, and
the mention of her name
leaves a sweet taste in
my mouth every time.

The Seductive Collection

Get Use to This

there will be
nowhere to run
and
no way to hide.

let your body
get used to this,
allow your body
to get used to me.

it doesn't matter
if you understand
why we met
and
why we feel
the way we feel
for each other.
let your body
get used to this,
allow your body
to get used to me.

don't be afraid
because it's
our first time.

let your body
get used to this,
allow your body

r. A. bentinck

to get used to me.
even if
you don't know how,
i'll show you.

let your body
get used to this,
allow your body
to get used to me.
it doesn't matter
where we are
the feelings will
remain the same.

let your body
get used to this,

allow your body
to get used to me.

The Seductive Collection

Time

time has a malicious way of
slipping away when
we are together.

time seems to lose
its value when we sit
in each other's company.

time seems to gain
tremendous value
when we are lost in each other.

it's astonishing how
we consistently lose track of time
whenever we speak.
with the wink of an eye
five and six minutes swiftly
turn into five and six hours.
every time we meet and speak
we invariably find ourselves
silently begging for more time,

wishing for more hours in the day,
afraid to look at the clock,

wanting more and more of
each other's company and warmth
while vanishing time nips at
our need to be together.

r. A. bentinck

Fiery

her coy exterior
is extremely deceptive,
she hides a bouquet
of sensual beauty
beneath it all.

her pleasant demeanour
is misleading.
she is a lot fierier
than i expected,

but in her fire
i wish to burn.

her stimulating imagination
can fondle your mind
in unimaginable ways,
her smile is inviting
and her eyes toy
with your delicate senses.

her selective words
take you to forbidden places
where you know its
wrong to indulge
but you have
no intentions of being right.

i am enticed by her fire.

The Seductive Collection

like a moth,
i want to dance in
the heat of her flame.
she is so much fierier
than i expected,
but i don't mind
burnin' in her insatiable flames.

r. A. bentinck

The Ease in Her Tease

unconsciously she teases
with effortless ease.

the graceful flow of
her tantalising body as
she featly walks away,

the consuming fire in
her penetrating stare,

the soothing sound of
her shy laughter
fondle with my ears.

she doesn't have
to do much to
quickly entice,
gently tease,
stealthy seduce
and
to naturally stimulate
the pleasurable excitement
in me.

she does it all
with unconscious ease.

The *Seductive* Collection

The Mysteries of You

i am lured by
the mysteries of you.

i want to know what
makes you smile so sweetly.

i want to know the thoughts
behind those penetrating looks
you give me frequently.

i am caught up in
the mysteries of you.

i am tempted by
the mysteries of you.

tell me what
turns you on,
tell me all
about your guarded fantasies,

tell me what makes you
quivers with unquenchable desires.

i am enraptured by
the mysteries of you.
i am enticed by
the mysteries of you.
show me what fuels

r. A. bentinck

your passionate yearnings,
show me the way to
your seductive sanctuary,

show me the way to
your secret sweet spot.

i am enthralled by
the mysteries of you.

The Seductive Collection

Wondering

i often wonder
what is going through
her mind
when words are
no longer useful

and
our breath
and
fingers speak
about what we are experiencing.

i oftentimes wonder
what's going through
her head when
she gives me
that indescribable look
which sends my emotions
on an instant high.

r. A. bentinck

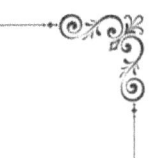

Inseparable

it's very arduous
to separate her
from
the joyful moments
of my days.

it's impossible
to go through the day
without something
reminding me of
her heavenly goodness.

she is an integral
part of all
my daily smiles,
my frequent laughter,
my blissful moments,
my countless inspirations,
and
my endless blessings.

The *Seductive* Collection

Morning Thoughts

it feels so good
waking up to
morning thoughts
of you.

thinking of
your charming smile that
melt my heart,

reflecting on your silly grin
when you are cheerful,

thinking about
your luscious kisses
and your irresistible lips,

contemplating the warmth of your
comforting embrace,
considering the hypnotic sensation
of your natural fragrance.

it always feels pleasant
waking up to thoughts
of you in the mornings.

r. A. bentinck

Kissology
(the anatomy of a kiss)

i get overwhelmed by
the amorous stupor
and
all my senses get activated
to this
one moment,
with these
multiplicities of sensations.

i watched her eyes
slowly close
and we drift off to
that place where
we began
to taste every flavour
on each other's tongue.

somehow i got to
the stage where
i could read
the messages in
her every breath,

where her hands
spoke a language too
complexed to be translated
into words

The Seductive Collection

but
simple enough
for my body
to comprehend.
her lips were
invigorating,

her tongue was
alluring,

her breath was
soothing

and
the fragrance
from her hair was
enticing.

we were both
blissfully lost in
this kiss-filled moment
where our kissing appetite
became insatiable
by the minute.

r. A. bentinck

Take Me There Again

take me to that place
where our breaths
become one,

take me to that place
where our lips
get entangled in a battle
that doesn't involve
retreating,
nor surrendering.

let's go to that place
where our embrace
is so close that even
the wind can't find
a way through.

take me to that place
where we don't need words
to communicate because
our body language
is so fluent that
interpretation is instantaneous
and all desires are satiated.

Mornings of Memories

there is nothing to compare
to waking up with
the fond memories
of her affectionate kisses
on my mind.

there is a freshness
that comes from reminiscing
about her delightful smile.

her morning memories
wake me up in
the sweetest of ways daily.

good morning,
morning memories.

r. A. bentinck

The Wind and Your Hair

i enjoy the way your hair
take flight in the wind
obediently dancing
to every rhythmic beat.

i love the fragrance
your hair releases
to the command of
the whispering wind.

i appreciate the way
the sun finds its way
through each wispy strand
lending rich colour
to your clustered beauty
in every way.

i enjoy the way the wind
play those tender games
with your hair,

one moment it tenderly
toss a few strands
concealing your eyes

and
every now and again
enough strands
to obscure your entire face,

The Seductive Collection

some strands are even
wise enough
to steal a kiss by
slipping through your lips.

i love the way you slowly
brush those disobedient
strands away with such
seductive ease.
i love the sight of your hair
blowing and flowing
in the wind.

r. A. bentinck

The look of love

you often ask,
why are you looking at me?

what are you searching for?

are you trying to study me?

i look into your eyes
because i am in love
with the way
you look at me.

i look into your eyes
because i am in love
with the way
your eyes caress me.

i look into your eyes
because i am in love with
the vibrations that
embrace me
whenever you look at me.

The Seductive Collection

Starvation

it's more than just missing
your sensually sweet kisses,
its more like
i'm starving.

if this is not
starvation
then please tell me
what is it?

you have me craving,
you have me day-dreaming,
you have me fantasing,
you have me reminiscing,

you have me starving
just because i yearn
for your kisses.
this is much
more than missing
your delectable kisses,

it's an emergency situation
that needs
your immediate attention.

r. A. bentinck

Forgive Me

please forgive me.
it was never my intention
to desire you this much.

forgive me, please.

i didn't know that
i would grow to
crave so much about you.

please, forgive me.

i didn't know that
your hugs would be
so warm and enticing,

i didn't know your fingers
would be this gentle and magical,
i didn't know your lips
would be this soft and irresistible.

i beg for your forgiveness.

it's not that i don't have self-control,
it's not that i would die without
all your goodness,
it's not like i cannot think of
anything else,
it's just too difficult

The Seductive Collection

at this time to pretend
that there is so much
about you to fall in love
with
over and
over again.
please forgive me
my weakness at this time.

r. A. bentinck

Those Eyes

they look at me
with such seductive tease,
your gorgeous eyes.

they caress me so tenderly
and so frequently,
your sweet eyes.

your eyes toys
with my emotions,
drives me up
against a wall of desires,

set my emotions afire,
leaves me with
insatiable desires.

those sensual eyes of yours.
you look at me in
so many expressive ways
and it doesn't matter
where or when

you still evoke those
gentle feelings that take
over me.

The *Seductive* Collection

Let Go and Let it Be

when will you let
yourself finally be free?

why won't you release
your bridled emotions?

what would it take for you
to give free rein to
your racy fantasies?

when will you leave
your fears behind and just be?

when will you let go
and be spontaneous with me?

let go of everything and just be.

r. A. bentinck

Expressive Eyes

her eyes are
very expressive.
with one look
she can undress me
in public
in her uniquely sly and
inconspicuous ways.

with her words
she can lie
but her eyes,
they never deceive.

her eyes can be
mischievously deceptive
at times.

they tell me stories
of her seductive thoughts.

her eyes seduce me,
her eyes tease me,
her eyes please me,
her eyes turn me on,
her eyes lead me on.

her eyes,
the things they can do
to my excited imagination.

The *Seductive* Collection

My Secrets

will you keep my secrets?

please don't tell my friends
that i lose my common sense
whenever i'm around you.

don't tell them i'm in the habit of
begging for more and more
of your sweetness.

please don't tell them
i love the freak in you dearly.

don't inform anyone that i can't
seem to keep my eyes off you.

please don't tell them i'm
a glutton for your precious kisses.
don't even mention
that i'm a sucker for your
delicious tongue.

please keep my secrets
between you and me.

r. A. bentinck

Tonight

i just feel like
chilling with you
all cuddled up
in my arms tonight,

while we count the stars
and listen to slow jams
playing softly in
the background.

tonight, i just want
to be with you
in that cool and
relaxing way

where the soft breeze
caress your hair
and i can feel
the warmth of your body
pressed against mine
and your aromatic fragrance
dances in my nose.

i just wanna be
with you tonight.

The Seductive Collection

Just Surrender

let my caresses
transport you
to places you have
never visited before

all i'm asking you
to do is just surrender, baby.

don't resist
your innate feelings,
don't bridle
your racing desires,

don't stifle
your troublesome yearnings.
just surrender.
let my caresses
usher you to the edge of
your insatiable hunger.

baby,
i'm pleading with you to
just surrender.

why are you trying to conceal
those sensual feelings?
what are you afraid of?
why won't you
just surrender?

r. A. bentinck

Stay a Little Longer

i cherish every moment
in your presence
but somehow
time never does us justice.

can you please
stay a little longer?

i enjoy the sound of
your laughing voice,
and i savour
the sweet warmth of
your affectionate embrace.

baby, please,
stay a little longer.

your kisses are priceless
and the gentle look in
your eyes i can't
seem to get enough.

baby, please
stay a little longer.

The Seductive Collection

This Moment

i was never told
that this moment
would be so special.

no one told me
that your sweet kisses
came with a combination
of all the right ingredients.

your smooth and supple lips
were like honey
glazed with extra sweetness.

your tongue spoke
the ultimate language
of pleasurable satisfaction.
your hungry fingers
took hold of my sensitive skin
and i can feel all
the emotions that are overflowing.

i was overwhelmed
by the purity and passion
of the moment
and in all, i could do
was wish it lasted
for more than just today.

r. A. bentinck

How I Want You

i want to feel you with
my hands in your hands
up against the wall
overcome with
inextinguishable emotions.

i want to hear your
loud moans and groans
because words are
too difficult to speak
in the heat of the moment.

i want you with
your eyes closed
as you get lost in the
overpowering desires of
this moment.

i want you with your nails
sinking into my flesh
as it cries out for mercy
yet still not wanting you
to stop.

i want you breathing
with fast and uncontrolled breaths
as your body wiggles
under the weight of
these sensual sensations.

The *Seductive* Collection

Waking Up To You

i want to wake up
to the memories of
my fingertips still
drenched with
your perspiration.

i want to wake up to
the sounds of the
morning bird and
the warmth of your body
blanketing mine.

i want to wake up
to the lingering aftertaste
of your tantalising tongue
still in my mouth.

i want to wake up
to the pleasant sounds
of your gentle breath
while i get lost
watching your sleeping eyes.

i want to wake up
to your aromatic fragrance
caressing each morning breath.

i want to wake up
with and to the memories of you.

r. A. bentinck

Running Around

i caught you today
running around
in my restless mind.

you were leaving traces
of your irresistible memories
all over again.

i saw the glow of your face
as we get lost
in a passionate kiss,

i heard your voice whispering to me
words that put my heart
in a sensual spin,

i watched you running around
in my mind today
and the footprints you leave
have me yearning
for more of you.

The *Seductive* Collection

Right Now

all i want
right now
is to feel
the warmth of
your pleasurable lips.

all i want
at this moment
is to feel your tongue
slowly fondling
my mouth.

all i want is
to look into
your dreamy eyes and
get lost in
your tender stare.

all i want
right now is
to be with you.

r. A. bentinck

Tomorrow

the day has just ended
and i am already thinking
about tomorrow with you.
today was a gift
wrapped up in your
lovely memories
and i can't wait
until tomorrow to do
it all over again.

when the night's sky
blanket the atmosphere
i count the hours
with excited anticipation
waiting for tomorrow
to come.

as sleep comes
quietly calling
i surrender to its urges
falling asleep with you and
tomorrow on my mind.

the day has just ended
and as i drift off to sleep
there is a satisfying smile
on my face
knowing that tomorrow
we will meet again.

The *Seductive* Collection

Heart on the Line

i lay in all out there
i am not
holding back!

i have decided to lay
my heart on the line.

i have placed
my strong emotions
and weaknesses
all on your table.

i have declared
my amorous intentions
and
i have shown you
the inside of
my flaming fantasies.
i have shown it all
to you.
i don't intend
to hold back my feelings,

i am placing it all
on the line
because i know the feelings
i have for you is true.

r. A. bentinck

Fluids

the slow and consistent build-up
of bodily fluids
told the true story of today.

we were soaked
with perspiration and
covered in a surplus of
unbearable body heat.

exploding sensuous juices
overflowed and glistened
the already slippery surface
of our burning skin.

today we rode
the slippery slope
of some intense emotions
and i am still recovering
from the electrifying experience.

Obedience

when i gravitate towards
your alluring eyes,
like a moth to the flame,

it's not an obsession
it's obedience.

when i give in to the call of
your wild and passionate side
and i get carried away
by the moment,

it's not an obsession
it's obedience.

at nights when i can't help
but give in to the temptations
of your unforgettable memories,
it's not an obsession,
it's obedience.

when kissing your luscious lips
and always wanting more
and more,
and more,
of those precious kisses,

it's not an obsession,
it's obedience.

r. A. bentinck

when caressing you
in an affectionate embrace
and i don't want to let go
too soon,

it's not an obsession,
it's obedience.

it's me being obedient
to all
that is ravishing
about you.

The *Seductive* Collection

The White T-shirt

she suddenly appeared
from behind the locked door.
clad in nothing but
a big white t-shirt.

there was something alluring
about watching her walk
with such effortless ease
in her favourite
big white t-shirt.

she had a broad smile
veiling her face and
her bare feet played
a tapping beat
as they romanced
the tarry walkway.

it was a sight to behold
an unforgettable one.
today i saw a seductress in
a big white t-shirt.

r. A. bentinck

Beautiful

wake up beautiful,
someone is thinking
about you
early in the morning
and it feels so good.

hello, beautiful,
someone is happy
to see you once again.

goodbye, beautiful,
someone will be
missing you
when you are away
even if it's for a day.

goodnight, beautiful,
someone will be
missing you
while you sleep,

someone will be dreaming
of you while you sleep,

someone will be wishing
for the morning
to come quickly just
to see all of your beauty
once again.

Lost in the Moment

with glazed eyes,
anticipatory desires and
lips that quiver
with pleasurable excitement,
we surrendered to the urgings
of a consuming kiss.

our breaths became one,
as our lips locked
in a heated battle
fueled by our mutual longings.

your fingernails
clawed into
the cotton fabric
penetrating my sensitive flesh;
it pains in a strangely
desirous way.

your body began
to speak a language
that makes me want
to find ways to
satisfy you even more.

r. A. bentinck

Do It Again

you know that thing
you did to me
with your tongue
the last time we kissed?

do it again!

you know the way
your fingers roamed
my body uncovering
and discovering
sensitive places while fueling
uncontrollable desires?

do it again!

you know that
soft desiring look
you always give me
just before we close our eyes
loss in a blissful kiss?

do it again!

you know
that moaning sound
you make every time
the feelings get overheated
and you get carried away

The Seductive Collection

on an amorous cloud?

do it again!
all the things you do
to take my breath and
inhibitions away
just do them all over again.

r. A. bentinck

Afraid

she warned me repeatedly,

*baby, i am afraid to
let go of these
surging urges.*

*i don't think
i will be able to
control my emotions
when i am with you.*

she paused then continued,

*if i let go
i will pin you to
the floor and i won't let you getaway.*

*i am afraid for you baby,
this is all new to me
and i don't know
what will happen,*

i am really afraid for you.

The *Seductive* Collection

Can't Get Enough

it's hard to get enough
of you, when each day
you get sweeter,

each day there is more
to discover,
more to savour,
more to delight in,
more to celebrate and treasure.

it's hard to get
enough of you,
when every day
in every way
you get sweeter
and more irresistible
by the hours.

r. A. bentinck

Forgetfulness

i backed her up
in the corner of
the room and
i devour her in
a deep and passionate kiss.

seconds felt like minutes
and minutes felt
like hours.

she pulled me closer,
held me tighter,
she had me in a
vice-like grip
as the sensation
flooded her body.

her breathing
changed pace and rhythms
and her breath became warm.

when we slowly retreated
she looked me deep
in my eyes and said softly,

you made me forget
how to breathe,
you caused me
to lose my breath.

The *Seductive* Collection

Playing with Her Fire

i can see the fire
in her eyes and
i can sense
the inherent dangers
of letting her in.

but i have the curiosity
of a child and
i want to discover and
learn more about
her seductive heat.

i want to play with
her flames.

so i let go and
let her in. it was one of
my boldest decisions yet
and every day
i get to savour her
in ways,
i didn't ever expect.

r. A. bentinck

Take Off Her Clothes

she kissed me tenderly,
she kissed me deeply,
she kissed me passionately,

now i can feel my fingers
urging me to take off
all her clothes.

when her tongue
plays with mine,
when her lips
touches mine,

when we get
lost in a sensuous kiss,
and i can feel her breath
burning her intentions
on my skin
i can hear my fingers whispering,
take off her clothes.

every time she
kisses me tenderly,
every time she
kisses me deeply,
every time she
kisses me passionately
i can sense my fingers
itching to take off all her clothes.

The *Seductive* Collection

Sensual Vibrations

it's in your relaxed and
piercing countenance,

it's in the slow parting of
your luscious lips that curve into
an irresistible smile,

it's in the twinkle of
your eager eyes
as we drift away in
an exploratory gaze,

it's in the ease of
your body language
that toys
with my carnal needs.
i can sense your desire
to connect on a deeper level,

i can feel your need
to have answers
to the many questions
running around in
your head.
i can detect
your thoughts
slowly romancing mine.
 i can perceive it all
in your sensual vibrations.

r. A. bentinck

She is the Reason

she is the reason for
my sweaty palms.
she is the reason for
my wrinkled sheets
and my shaking knees.

she is the reason for
the fire in my loins,
she is the reason for
the beads of perspiration
trickling down my spine.

she is the reason for
the smile on my face.
she is the reason for
the aching i feel
in my heart.

she is the reason why
i sleep like a baby
some nights and
she the reason why
i am up late at night because
loneliness is giving me a fight.

The *Seductive* Collection

When I Say...

when i say i love you
i am not talking about
the cookie-cutter kinda love,

when i say i love you
it means i will walk
with you on those
arduous days when
your feet hurt and
everything pains
in an uncomfortable way.

when i say i love you
i am not talking about
the kinda love that lust
off of your body,
i am talking about
a love that appreciates you,
body and soul,
where i take the time
to worship you and
your spirituality.

when i say i love you
it's not the selfish kinda love,
it's the kind of love
that allows me to know
when to shut up and
listen to you even when

r. A. bentinck

i want to speak,
it's the kinda love
that allows me to sit
with you in your silence
as we listen to the
wisdom of
the whispering wind.

it's that kinda love.
when i say i love you
it means on cold evenings
when it gets extremely frigid
i will give you
the t-shirt off my back,

i will give you the warmth
of my skin and
i will embrace you
so close that
the chilly breeze will be
left out in the cold.

when i say i love you
i am not talking about
the cookie-cutter kinda love,

it's love on a deeper level,
love on a deeper vibration,

a love that
will fight with you,
a love that
will fight for you
against your psychological demons,

The Seductive Collection

against your forgettable past,
a love that will love you
beyond and despite
your faults and scars,

a love that will cherish you
just because you are you.

r. A. bentinck

You're My Poetry

i get lost in your racy rhythm
time after time.
you draw me in
with your seductive smiles
and i am seduced
by your similarities
to so much in nature.

you capture me with
your metaphors and i surrender
to their endless temptation.

your imagery arouse
my senses and lead
me to wide-open fields
without no fences,
there my imagination runs free.

i sail away with
your rhymes and
in a unique way
they make me feel so fine.

i am overwhelmed
by your superb hyperboles
that embodies the essence of
you and me.
each day in so many ways
you are my daily dose of poetry.

The Seductive Collection

Connecting Spots

my tongue gently
traces lines connecting
the all the sensitive spots
on your erogenous zones.

i do it with one objective
in mind,
savouring the sounds of
your exploding ecstasy.

my tongue searches
each raised pores
on the surface of your
aroused skin
looking for your weak places

to tease you
to the point
of no retreat.

i do this with
one objective in mind,
blowing the covers
off your inhibitions
and setting
your imprisoned desire free.

r. A. bentinck

Daydreams

you are the fantasies
in my forbidden daydreams,

you are the fuel that ignites
the fire in my sensual soul.

when i am with you
i forget the world
and its troubles
while we drift away
in sweet ecstasy.

you are the fantasy
that takes me to places
i have never been before,

where no limitations exist
and i am free to be me.
you give me reasons
to ask for more:

more of what you give me,
more of what you bring to my life,
more of what we create together.

you are the main feature
in my eyes-wide-open
recurring dreams.

Is This Really You?

is this really you?
are those your eyes
smiling back at mine?

is this you?
is this your tongue
wrestling with mine
with such effortless ease?

is this really you?
is that your out-of-control breathing
that's warm against my neck?

is this you?
is this your hipbone
bumping and grinding
against mine
in unison to our sensual rhythms?

is this really you?
are you sure you are the innocent
soft-spoken girl, i know?

all this time
you were in front of me
i didn't see any of this
in you. just before you go
i have one request,
can you grind on me some more?

r. A. bentinck

Just One Moment

all it takes is one moment,
one fleeting moment
when we choose to surrender
to the callings of
our ever blazing desires.

there is no better place
to be,
there are no better feelings
to feel,
there are no better sounds
to hear
than our sounds of satiation.

all it took was one moment

to take us away
on a journey
so sweet, so seductive,
so mind-blowing,
so pure,
so filled with the
ideal chemistry.

all it takes is one moment
for us to take flight
on feelings so high
we can touch the clouds.

The Seductive Collection

Listen

i'm listening
to the rain
on the tin roof
as it complements
this moment beautifully.

i'm listening
to our heartbeats
racing in tune
with the sounds we create
as we make love all day.

our favourite music
is set on repeat
as we tuned in
to its rhythmic beat
and sensual lyrics.

listen to the rhythms
we make when
hips speak the same
language and bodies wrestles
unrestricted.

listen to the music
we create as we savour
the essence of this
unforgettable moment.

r. A. bentinck

Seducing You

one of these days
i will sneak up from
behind you

while you are in deep
concentration
doing your work
and i will
fondle your apples
and
play with your cherries.

as usual,
you will
find a plausible reason
to stop me.
to interrupt my flow.
to slow me down
and
tell me to cool out.

but i in
my usually unique way
will find ways to convince
you to play along.

i will find a way
to make your juices flow,
i will find a way

The Seductive Collection

to make you ask for more,
i will find a way
to make you say
with that hungry look
in your eyes…

*DON'T YOU DARE
STOP NOW!*

r. A. bentinck

The Taste of You

you are beyond
irresistible.

you have
long gone pass
succulent.

you are more
like hot chocolate
drizzled with
extra honey-
sweeter than sweet!

you leave
an indelible
aftertaste in
my mouth
you keep my imagination
active.

your memories are
like strong coffee
that keeps me
up late at night.

you leave a flavour
so divine.
i am left with
a constant yearning

The Seductive Collection

for more of you.
you are more than
satisfying,
you are more than
mouthwatering,

you are more than
a hunger.
you are more like
nutrients,

an exquisite meal,
a thirst-quencher
a long and satisfying glass
of cold fruit juice
on a sweltering
summer's day.

r. A. bentinck

Smouldering

i am still feeling
the heat you left
in me from our last escapade.

i am still surrounded by
your sweet memories
every hour of the day.

i am still turned on
by your enticing imagery
and mind teasing ways.

i can still taste
the flavours of you
on the tip of
my tongue.

i can still smell
the essence of you
in every way,
your scent still lingers
in the halls of
my nostril.

i am still smouldering
from all the heat
you left on me
and with me from
the last time we met.

The *Seductive* Collection

Stealing Breaths

the closer we get
the more sultry
we become,
the closer we get
the more enticing
the moments become.

somehow the way
you touch me
always manages
to slowly steal my breath away.

somehow the sensuality
of your touches
always finds away
to make me
lose control.

you take me to places
that makes me
want to stay in
your presences
in an indefinite way.

the closer i get to you
the more i want you,
the closer i get to you
the sweeter each moment becomes.

r. A. bentinck

It's You and Me Tonight

tonight,
it's all about
you and me
under a blanket
of glittering stars.

tonight,
it's you and me
lying on
the convenient rocks
as our mattress
and a plump pillow.

tonight,
we will savour
the melodic music of
the whispering wind
and enjoy
each sweet and
welcoming caress.

tonight,
it's you and me
making music
as we dance to
the distinctive sounds of
our soft moaning.

tonight,

The Seductive Collection

we will get lost
in the gentle lullabies
of the splendid moon
as she slyly watches
over us with
glowing approval.

tonight,
we will give in
to our voracious urges
surrendering meekly
to what comes naturally.

r. A. bentinck

My Love

i want my love
to be the place you
come to for comfort
when it all gets too
crazy out there.

i want my love
to be the rag you use
to dry your weeping eyes
when life pains you
in unexplainable ways.

i want my love to be your shelter
from the relentless storm when there
is no port in sight.

i want my love
to be the blanket
you snuggle up
under when it gets
too cold outside.

i want my love
to be the guiding light
in your darkest hours
when you think
there is no hope left.
i want my love
to be a safe place you run to.

The Seductive Collection

My Inspiration

i pride myself in being
skilled in expressing myself,
to the extent that
i am seldom at a loss for words.

then you came
into my life
and all of a sudden
i am struggling
to find the right
combination of words
to describe the blessings
you bring.

now, all my poetry is
centred around you,
all my rhymes
are about you,

all my metaphors
celebrate you,
all my similes
enshrine you.

you stroll into my life
and suddenly
all the inspirations
i ever needed,
i found in you.

r. A. bentinck

you are the muse
that inspire my thinking,
you are the muse
that motivates my writing,

you are the muse
that is my everyday inspiration.

The *Seductive* Collection

Acoustic Love

she serenades me
by playing on my emotional strings
with her tantalizing words,
leaving a satisfying echo
in the corridor of my ears.

she strums on the cords
of my desires
with her delicious tongue
saturating
my insatiable longings.

she makes me
weak in the knees
with her pulsating tease
that energizes
all of my sensual faculties.

she knows how to bait me
with her smooth and lyrical words...

she said to me,
let's make music
with our tongues while
our bodies grind
to the rhythm
of our overheated strings.

r. A. bentinck

Sunrise

you are like
the sunrise teasingly
peeking over
the horizon line,

flooding the earth
with your
dazzling brightness,
poetic beauty,
and
refreshing rays.

you are like
the sunrise tenderly kissing
the fertile earth
softly

smiling with
a certain sweetness
instantly adding
your golden light
to the birth
of a new day.

you are like
the sunrise
you shine
your unconditional love
for all to see and feel.

The Seductive Collection

Poolside Beauty

her magnificent smile
and magical eyes
were the fuel
that turned on
my sensual engine.

this poolside beauty
had some
breathtaking qualities
that was complimented
by her
red two-piece bikini
and playful personality.
her tempting smile
and tantalizing eyes
were the accelerator
that revved
my emotional engine.

this poolside enchantress
had some mind-altering qualities
that was so magnetising
you couldn't help
but surrender to
the urge to stare
for a prolonged period.

r. A. bentinck

Sweet Sensations

the delightful sensations
gently steered her
to the seductive sanctuary,

transporting her away
from her familiar
and dull comfort space.

gradually she surrendered
to the irresistible urges
of this sensual environment.

and one by one
her unfulfilled fantasies
were satisfyingly fulfilled.

his spicy words,
the choice wine,
the flowing water,
her wicked intentions,
and
her seductive juices
that flowed generously

all contributed
to the satisfying look
plastered on her now
glowing face.

The Seductive Collection

Indescribable

if i genuinely knew
all
the pleasant words
in the comprehensive
english dictionary

i will still struggle
to find
the satisfactory combinations
to describe how exceptional
you looked today.

i was floored
by your regal elegance,
stimulated
by your sexiness,
captivated
by the graceful way
you moved and

genuinely impressed
by how effortless
your poetic beauty
brilliantly illuminated the room.

r. A. bentinck

Sleepless

her memories,
they always find a way
to sneak into my dreams
waking me up,

leaving me
panting for elusive breath,
searching for fresh air,
and with a strong desire
to be in her presence.

my sleep
is frequently interrupted
by her steamy memories
toying with
my insatiable need
for the satisfaction
only she can bring.

she seems to always
find a way into my dreams
in affectionate and teasing ways.

The *Seductive* Collection

Overthinking

don't
overthink it, baby,
just go with the flow.

don't fight
your genuine feelings
just open the door
to your alluring desires.

release
your fears and inhibitions
and let's lay it all out
on the floor.

don't
overthink it
you will ruin
our natural rhythms,
don't
overthink it
let's surrender
to the mutual hunger
that dominates the room.

r. A. bentinck

On the Cheek

she reached out to me
with pleasant hands
and delicate but electrifying fingers
caressing my cheek affectionately.

indescribable sensations
pulsed through my veins
while instantly delivering bolts
of pleasurable emotions
awakening all
of my repressed amorous wishes.
she leaned over casually
and faintly pecked me
on my blushing cheek.

the tempting warmth
of her lush lips
entered my pores and core,
and a swift storm
of pulsating emotions
instantly seized my body
and i became vulnerable
to the desire to hold her close.

she has these mischievous
and girlish ways
of making me senseless
with lustful desires
to be with her.

The Seductive Collection

Hard_to Get

i quietly reach to the sky
with a sneaky intention
to steal the stars just for you
but you won't give me a try.

i started to count the grains of sand
on the beach just to impress you
but you won't give me
the time of the day.

i went to the well
with a teaspoon just to fill
your empty barrel
and even that didn't please you.

i walked a thousand miles
bare feet
in the sweltering heat,
on the unforgiven asphalt,

my scorched feet told
the real story,
still, you won't give me
your time and attention.

what must i do to please you?

r. A. bentinck

A Ballad for the Broken
(to My Sisters with Love)

she is an earth angel
who carries her natural beauty
with effortless simplicity.

but they have hurt her
so she doesn't trust love
anymore.

sister, please come home to love.

someone smeared her innocence
in her tender years and squashed
the petals of her fragile flower.

now she is on a hurting mission
and
she will take no prisoners.
she doesn't care about love
and she doesn't want to be loved.

sister, please come home to love.

her trust in men
has been compromised
now she finds it hard to believe
and give in to her natural feelings.
her sexiness causes the thermometer

The Seductive Collection

to explode but her heart
is cold as below zero.

sister, please come home to love.
her hands are soft as a baby's cheek
but her caress is as hard
as greenheart wood.
she has been badly treated
and repeatedly molested
now she finds it too complex
to trust her tenderness.

sister, please come home to love.

her gentle tears struggle
to penetrate her steely eyes.
she has cried a thousand tears before
in silent places but always manages
to fake a smile for the world.
she is hurting daily
in places she rather not tell.

sister, please come home to love.
i stand in her pain
for a fleeting moment
and empathy hurts like a bitch!
but she carries this hurt daily
and often the painful memories
come calling, softly but brutally.

sister, please come home to love.

if my unrepentant brothers can
only see the deep and long-lasting

r. A. bentinck

scars and pains they subjected
our sisters to
will they ever change?
will they rearrange their foolish ways?
will they ever open their eyes
to see?

brothers let's please help
our sisters come home to love.
please.

The Seductive Collection

Closer

come a little closer,
i want to whisper in your ears.

i have some things to say
that i don't want the rest
of the world to hear.

i want to tell you about
the things i want to do with you
and the places i want to take
your imagination.

come a little closer,
i want to tell you about
my secret intentions,
my wickedest desires,
and how much you set
me on fire every time i see you.

come closer,
i want to smell
your sweet fragrance,

i want to hold you close,
i want to feel your breath
on my skin and
i want to squander the time away
in your sweetness.
just come a little closer.

r. A. bentinck

Don't Go

baby, please don't go yet.
if you leave me now
my thoughts of you
would have me up all night
and loneliness will
give me a severe fight.

please, baby, don't go just yet.

baby, if you leave now
i will lose my mind
sitting in the dark
thinking about no one else
but you.

please, baby don't go.
baby, please don't get
tired of me
asking you to stay
a little longer.

don't get tired of me
asking you to squeeze me
a little tighter.
don't get tired of me
wanting more and more
of your celestial sweetness.
please, baby, don't go just yet,
stay a little longer.

The *Seductive* Collection

A Little Longer

give me the little
you can give me now.

i will take the peck
on the cheek,
instead of the marathon
kissing session.

i will take the short
but affectionate embrace
instead, of our usual
prolonged hugs.

i will take the gentle
holding of hands
instead of walking
hand in hand aimlessly.

but,
i am not prepared
to wait another day
to hold and kiss you,

i am not prepared
to lose another precious moment
with you.

the periods of my life
when you are not around

r. A. bentinck

feel like one big void, a chasm
that's impossible to fill,
it feels like an eternity.
somehow this feels
like we are moons away.
i am accustomed to having
all of you,
i am accustomed to having you
in your favourite places
and in your preferred positions.

baby, desiring you
is something i have done
so long
now it's a hard habit to alter.

please stay a little longer.

The Seductive Collection

Hush

hush,
don't say another word,
hush baby.
your eyes are telling me
the whole story,
let me listen.

i can see your lust-filled
desires in your glistening eyes,
i can see your hunger
that needs satisfying,
i can read every thought
that you are trying
to hide.

hush baby,
don't say another word
i know just what i need
to do.
let me lead
and you just follow.

let me set the pace
and all you have
to do is keep up
with me.

let me create the conditions
that is conducive to your

r. A. bentinck

total satisfaction.
let me provide
the solutions for all
that i see in your
revealing eyes.

hush baby,
don't say another word,
i know just what to do.

The *Seductive* Collection

Cornered

she stepped into
the crowded room
and i silently exclaimed,

good god have mercy on me.

she rearranged my level
of self-confidence,
snatched the breath from
right under my nose
and instantly started up
a musical orchestra
on the walls of my chest.

her perfume captured me
in a way that left me
transfixed on her
in a ghostly daze.
when she stepped
into the room
i was at the mercies
of all her royal splendour.

she was an angel
in stilettoes, a temptress
in silk fitted dress,
and the reason for
my now weakened knees
and scattered thoughts.

r. A. bentinck

Remembering

my hands
they remember
what you felt like.

my eyes cannot
get rid of the essence
of your radiant beauty,

my nostrils
remember your irresistible
natural fragrance,

and

my ears still echo
with the soothing sound
of your capturing voice.

The Seductive Collection

I Won't

just because
i could
doesn't mean
i would.

i won't
fall for
your sweetness,
no.
i won't
give into
your sultry ways.

i won't
beg you
to stay when
you are about
to leave,
i won't
think about
your loveliness
when i can't seem
to get any rest.

just because
i could
doesn't mean
i would.
i won't

r. A. bentinck

follow
your temptation trail,
i won't
salivate at
your dining table,

i won't
drool over
your dripping honey.

despite all
your irresistibility
i refuse to give in
to you and all
your immeasurable splendour.

The *Seductive* Collection

Not a Player

no,
i am not a player.
never has and
never will be one.

but, i do understand
your love language.

don't envy my fluency,
in the way i interpret
your every need,

don't begrudge
my smooth ways
it's just my natural way
of responding to
your countless blessings.

no, i am not a player.
i never was and never will be.

i am only an obedient
observer who is
humbly responding
to your irresistible
love pheromones.
no, i am not a player.
i am not into
playing any games.

r. A. bentinck

Sitting and Watching
(Egotistic)

i am sitting here
watching you
making a fool of yourself.

you know
i'm gonna get you
don't you?

quit the girlish games.

i will sit here
and watch you
run till you get tired,

i will be right here
waiting
when you have come
to realize that loving me
is the only way,
and has always
been the only way.

i'll be right here waiting
while you fight against
what you feel
so naturally.
i'll be here to feed

The Seductive Collection

your hunger,

i'll be here
to quench
your emotional thirst
i'll be
sitting right here.

i'll be right here
waiting for you
when love leads you
my way.

i'll be here
come what may.

how long do you intend
to run,
to hide,
to disguise,
to play
your silly game.

how long?

r. A. bentinck

Oohs and Ahs

i have grown to
appreciate deciphering
her language of pleasure.

it's evident in
the sounds she makes
that speaks
of insane satisfaction.

her english tongue
get confused and
she resorts to speaking in
oohs and aahs as
a sign of
her pleasurable approvals.

The *Seductive* Collection

Heartbeat

why does your presence
manipulate my heartbeat
this much?

one thought of you
and my heart gallops
like wild horses
running free.

why the anticipation
of holding you in my arms
send shivering sensations
throughout my body?

when your lips meet mine
my heart beats at a speed
that's unfamiliar to me.
when you are far away
my heart rate slows
to a sad and dreary rhythm
and my emotions run cold.

why does your presence
control my heartbeat
this much?

r. A. bentinck

On the Dance Floor

she is courteous and respectful
in person. the sweetest and most
charming personalities
to be around.
but when she gets
on the dance floor
she instantly mutates into
a sultry goddess.

her once petite
and decent waste line
become a gyrating and
grinding machine.
her rhythmic moves are flawless
and she drops dance moves
that makes your mouth water
and your loins boil
with fierce desires.

her expanding waistline speaks
a dance language that simple
to interpret but difficult
to erase from the overactive mind.

she is a lady in daily life
but on the dance floor
she is a tantalising sensation
that leaves you weak in the knees and
drenched with perspiration.

The *Seductive* Collection

A Sweet Discovery
(for Neelam)

from nowhere it seems
she stumbled upon
my poetic words,
then she found her way
into my thoughts,
and finally into my literary life.

her pleasant countenance
is sweet and succulent,
the gentle vibrations
she exudes
elevate the spirit
and sets me free from
the chains melancholy.

her pictures scream
classy royalty,
her regal elegance
is a splendid sight to behold
and something to cherish
dearly.

we are separated by
seas and continents
but that's doesn't restrict us
from generously sharing
mutual respect and friendship.

r. A. bentinck

i wait for the day
to bask in the glow
of her dazzling radiance.
we might be miles between
seas and continents but
this has turned out to be such
a sweet discovery.

The *Seductive* Collection

The Passing Smile

it was right there
in her
passing smile.

the irresistible allure,
the pulsating sensations,
the spine-tingling blessings,
the heartbeat elevators.

it was all there,
right there in her
passing smile.

r. A. bentinck

Caged Scream

her controlled persuasion
held me in
frozen anticipation.

her precise attention
to meticulous details
tease me to
the edge of my
already frazzled self-control.

i am trying my best
not to explode.

her electrical fingers
shock me to the core
i am holding on for
dear life,
but i can only do it
for so long.

the ear-shattering scream
breakthrough the barriers
and the neighbourhood
is set alight by
my exploding
sounds of satisfaction.

The *Seductive* Collection

Bliss

the
lazy stroll
of
clouds overhead,

the
sweet sway of
your flowing skirt
in
the afternoon breeze,

your
wispy hair dancing
to the rhythms of the wind,

the
seducing ring
of your silky voice in my ear
makes this afternoon
so much sweeter.

r. A. bentinck

Comfort Zone

nestled in the comfort
of your abiding memories
i drifted off in a reverie.

i slowly drift away
in the bosom of asleep
so soft and sweet,

with a smile painted
on my relaxed face,
sweet dreams,
here i come.

The *Seductive* Collection

Connecting Dots

i have developed
the art of
connecting the dots
from her head
to her pinkie toe.

i know-how
to find
the right routes
on her spine to generate
the ideal sensations.

i know how to draw
the lines between
her lips
and
her hips.

i know the intensity
and the amount
of pressure, i need to apply
on each of her pleasure points.

i have become a skilled
dot connector
every time i am with her.

r. A. bentinck

Ember

the fiery screams
and
intense moans
have subsided finally.

the fierce flames
in our loins
doesn't blaze as intensely
as before.

our weary bodies
sprawled in
the after-effects of
dying seductive embers.

emotions smoulder
in the glowing ashes of
crumpled fabric.
we lay there
staring into each other's eyes
speechless but satisfied.

Embrace

i can feel the
magical vibes
instantly transferring
from her inner being
to mine.

her gentle hands,
soft and sensitive
write unspeakable
emotions on my
alert senses.

she clutches me
in an affectionate embrace
and
i can feel
the private thoughts
she's thinking
and i can tell

she wants me
just as much as
i want her.

r. A. bentinck

Sipping Her Lips

i took a sip of
her wine and tasted
the irresistible essence of
her lips on
the rim of the crystal vessel.

in offering me
a sip of her wine
she inadvertently
gave me a taste
of her delectable lips.

with that single sip
i am left with an
instant yearning
to taste the real ambience
of her soft and sensual
petal lips.

The Seductive Collection

Footprints

i just love how
you leave
angelic footprints
and
dainty memories
in my life
every time we meet.

you tiptoe
with feather-like steps
in the hallways of
my mind
leaving traces of
celestial blessings
behind.

r. A. bentinck

Her Hands

she held my hands
and i felt complete.
the soft and gentleness
of her palm
said to me what
words could
never say.

she held my hand
while we sauntered
in the pouring rain
and

the essence of
her tenderness
seeped into my pores
saying,
things will never be
the same after today.

The *Seductive* **Collection**

Her Memories

her pleasant memories
are like a thermal blanket
on a frigid
solitary evening.

in a comfortable bed,
with unfavourable
plump pillows
for my company
i wander off to meet
her engaging and
unforgettable memories.

her fond memories
were like a sincere
and welcoming blanket
on a bleak and chilly
quiet evening.

r. A. bentinck

Hostage

your teeth are holding
my tongue hostage.

in the excitement
of the moment
she lost control
and
you give in to
her primal urges.

suddenly biting me.

now my tongue is
the innocent victim
of your unbridled emotions.

The *Seductive* Collection

How?

we got engrossed
in the moments and
time crept by,

we were trapped
in a bodily cocoon,
and
the only thing
that mattered was us.

how did the bed
manage to
get this wet?

when did
the pillows
fall to the floor?
what caused us
to lose all
sense of control?

we both looked
at each other
with questioning eyes

but neither of us
had the courage
to say what we were thinking.

r. A. bentinck

Hummingbirds and Bees

i wanna be like
the hummingbirds and
the bees.

i wanna develop
that innate sense
to be able to savour
the sweet bounty of
your glorious nectar.

i wanna be like
the hummingbirds and
the bees.

i wanna be saturated
in your pollen
taking your
aromatic fragrance
with me everywhere.
i wanna be like
the hummingbirds and
the bees.

i wanna be skilled enough
to extract your delicious nectar
without breaking
or smearing
your delicate petals.
i wanna be like

The *Seductive* Collection

the hummingbirds and
the bees.
i wanna be the sole possessor
of the skills to access
all your precious sweetness
daily.

r. A. bentinck

If I Follow

if i follow
my heart i will
fall for you.

if i follow
these feelings
i will fall head
over heels with you.

if i follow
your lure i will
lose my moral grounding.

but if i don't
follow i will
chastise me for letting you go.

The *Seductive* Collection

Infliction

i was quiet in
my humble corner
then you came by
and
inflicted me with passion
so elevating.

you infected me
with a lust-filled disease
now am always
wanting more of you.

r. A. bentinck

No Comparison

i am trying to find things
to compare to the feelings
i get when i'm with you.

butterflies arrive
in abundance,
nervousness pays
an untimely visit,

temptations wouldn't
leave me alone.

nothing else can compare
to the things i feel
when i'm with or
around you.

The *Seductive* Collection

Paradoxical

she forewarned me
in a stern tone,

*i come with
my own complications.*

*i'm a good girl with
lots of naughty tendencies,
can you efficiently handle me?*

i stood there
with a beaming grin
and a racing mind
wondering if i am capable
of handling
this apparent paradox
of a woman.

then
she disturbs
my thoughts process
with another question.
can you handle
all of this goodness?

r. A. bentinck

Fantasising

i will not lie,
i am fantasising about you
right now.

i am
looking at your full lips
and my thoughts are
taking me to places
where i can see you
do things to me
with those sexy lips.
girl, i am fantasising about you.

i see your curvy hips
and my desires pinned
me to the floor and
i can visualise
your rhythmic motions
as you bump and grind
uncontrollably.
baby, i am fantasizing about you.

i smell the uplifting scent
of your natural fragrance
and i drift away in a reverie
about you and me.
baby, i am caught up in
a fantasy about you
and it feels really good.

The Seductive Collection

Cravings

*why do you
have to go now?*

his inquiry interrupted
her teasing steps.

*please stay
a little longer.*

he pleaded with
desiring eyes and
an uncontrollable loin.

slowly,
she returned,
looked at him
with alluring eyes,
and butterfly kissed him
on the forehead,
then softly whispered,

*i can't stay much longer
i have to go.
bye, sweetie.*

r. A. bentinck

Feast on Me

unleash your inner temptress.

throw away
your inhibitions
and let's get wild!

let your imagination
roam the undiscovered
sensual fields
and just feast on me.

open your eyes
and don't be shy,
see all there is
to see
and just feast on me.

Indecent Proposal

are you afraid to eat it?

he stood there speechless
with a guilty
yet startling smile
plastered on his face.

nope!
(he was lying)
he replied nervously.

*i want you to eat it
like an ice cream cone
on a hot summer's day,*

she said with a face
flooded with confidence
and excited anticipation.
*don't play around,
eat it like you want it,
eat it like you are starving.*

r. A. bentinck

Intentions

from the very first time
i laid eyes on you i knew
what i wanted
from you
and
what i wanted
to do with you.

my intentions
were vivid in my mind.

from the very first time
i held you close
in a friendly embrace
i knew what i felt
for you
and
about you.
my intentions
and feelings were
very clear.

i want all of you,
give me all of you.

The *Seductive* Collection

Flirty

She tightens
the screws
on her tease
and
i pleaded to her.

i begged for more,
i asked her not to go,

i pleaded for her
not to stop,
i try to get her
to slow down

i told her not
to make so much noise.
then she intensified
the heat in her charm
and i was swarmed
by stinging emotions.

i am now a slave
to her unspoken temptations.

they say to me,
come get me,
please come take me.

r. A. bentinck

Lights

the softness of the blue disco lights
clothed your sensational curves.

Quincy Jones *'The Secret Garden'*
took control of our emotions
and we moved to the
commanding lyrics
and each seductive beat.

on a crowded dancefloor
you were the only one i saw,
you were the only one i needed.
and as the lyrics took hold of us
all i could hear was,

"i need to be with you let me lay beside you
do what you want me to all night
gonna hold you, ooh baby, can i touch
you there"

we were both caught up in
the rapture of the moment
and the dim disco lights
provided the perfect complement
to the smooth voice of Barry White's request,

"tonight i want to learn all about
the secrets in your garden."

The Seductive Collection

Reservation

bartender,
turn down your lights
and pour my baby
a glass of fine red wine.

please put on some
Teddy Pendergrass
and leave us undisturbed.

this is a reservation
just for two.

bartender,
please turn down your lights
just a little lower
and pour my baby
another glass
of that special wine,
go on and leave us alone
this is a reservation for two.

r. A. bentinck

Unplanned

i didn't see this coming.
there is no way
i could have planned
any of this.

the slow burn,
the heat of the moment,
the fire in our eyes,
the insatiable calls
of wild desires,
the pleasurable sounds
and,
your kisses of ecstasy.

we didn't have what it
take to plan all of this
the way it turned out to be.
i couldn't see this coming.

The Seductive Collection

Woman Enough

i don't want you
to be worried about me.

i'm woman enough
to deal with all that
you want to give to me.

don't hold back,
don't slow down,
don't go easy on me.

i'm woman enough
to take all you have
and can give to me.

don't be shy,
don't tell me any lies,
just give it to me straight.
i'm woman enough
to hear all
your nefarious thoughts.

give it to me,
i'm woman enough
to take it all.

r. A. bentinck

The Dirty Looks

she signalled
her wicked intentions
with a prolong
and intense dirty look.

she held me tenderly
by the hands
and tossed me
onto the welcoming bed,

and proceeded
to satisfy her
overwhelming needs
in a selfish way
that left me speechless.

The Seductive Collection

Playful Lips

her rosy lips are
like licking
freshly spread butter
from a slice of bread-
silky smooth.

it's flushed and tender
like the petals
of dew-kissed rose.

when her pleasant words flow
you get lost in
the ineffable sweetness
of every word she says.

her lips have a way of
taunting you,
delighting you,
inviting you,
engaging you,

in ways that leave
you enthralled.

r. A. bentinck

Wanting It All

call me greedy.
call me a glutton.
call me covetous.

i don't care!
i desire all of you.

all your smiles.
all of your laughter.
all of your alluring smells.
all of your goodness.

call me greedy.
call me a glutton.
call me covetous.
i don't care,
give me all of you.

The *Seductive* Collection

Playful Torture

i will torture you
slow and easy
with my pleasure tease.

i will take you
to the depths
of your rebellious
desires and release
you to the mercies
of their taunting.

i will take you to
the precipice of
intense pleasure
and expose your
vulnerabilities
and
i will be there
to fulfill all your
aching unfulfilled longings
and satisfy your need
to be pleased.

r. A. bentinck

Beautiful

your celestial gifts
merge beautifully
with your intellectual wit.

you turned on
your sunlight smile
and i'm enticed
by its ever-present rays.

you define
a rare kind of beauty,
one that few possess
and
many pray for.
you radiate natural beauty
effortlessly.

The Seductive Collection

Close to You

it's the only place
i love to be
when i'm with you,
close to you.
it's the only way
i can smell
your aromatic fragrance
that puts me in a trance,
close to you.

it's the only time
i get the chance to
stare into your
gorgeous brown eyes
and get lost inside of your dream,
close to you.

it's the only moment
i get the opportunity
to bask in the glow of
your radiant smile,
close to you.
being close to you
is the place i love to linger
for eternity and take in all of
your sweet blessings.

being close to you
is where i love to be.

r. A. bentinck

Earth Angel

she protects herself
with an exterior
that is
fiery,

but beneath
the projected heat
lies
her concealed gems.

eyes
that caresses you
so softly,
a smile
that seeps into
your heart
quietly lighting
it up with
unspeakable joys,
and
laughter that engages
your attention
in a way
that chases
your blues away.

The *Seductive* **Collection**

The Reason

you are the kind of girl
the stars come out for
on a lovely night.

you are the reason
the moon shines so brightly
in a clouded night sky.

you are the reason
the sun still shines
behind the gloomy skies.

and
you are the reason
why these days seem
so much longer and sweeter.

r. A. bentinck

After You

after you kissed me
it feels like i've been
kissed for the first time.

after you made love to me
it felt like i made love
for the very first time.

when you touched me
the electricity that courses
through my veins
felt like i've been
touched for the first time.

after sharing
and experiencing
all of you
it seems like there
will be no one after you.

The *Seductive* Collection

In My Arms
(T.L.C.)

in my arms is
where you need to be.
i wanna cradle
your passionate hunger
and fuel your explosive fantasies.

in my comforting arms is
where you rightfully belong.
i wanna eliminate
your familiar fears
and fertilise the fields
for your unfulfilled needs
to grow.

in my protective arms is
where you should be.
i wanna embrace
your gentle warmth
and chase all
your blues away.

in my soothing arms is
where you should be.
i wanna taste the ineffable sweetness
of your honey while
savouring the glowing embers
of your burning flames.

r. A. bentinck

The Taste of Love

you are undoubtedly
what love taste like

you are precisely
what love feels like

you are genuinely
what love smells like

you are typically
what love sounds like.

in an unforgettable way
you embody
the true essence of
a natural love.

The Seductive Collection

Your Fire

i am on fire and no one
can douse my flames
but you.

no one could have prepared me
for the heat generated
by your flames.

you burn me in places
i never thought
could be reached.

what is the source of
your fiery passion?

my quenchless desires
are consumed
by your eternal blaze.

r. A. bentinck

You Are the Reason

it's because of
charming women like you
why sweet and happy
songs are sung.

it's attractive women
like you
that contributes
to the superb writing of
timeless love classics.

women like you
fuel the fierce fire of
erotic poetry and
sultry poetic language.

you are the prime reason
and the principal meaning
in every pleasant word,

every memorable line,
every soothing rhyme,

and every evocative imagery
in all my creations.

The *Seductive* Collection

There is a Reason

it might be
the things that
you do
or
it might be
the things that
you say.

there is a reason
why i feel
this way.

your consistent effects
on me
keeps me
holding on,
keeps me
going strong,
keeps me
yearning
for you more.

r. A. bentinck

When You Smile

when i see you smile
countless butterflies
take control of my body,

my imagination takes wings
and am enticed by
a multiplicity of feelings
that awakens in
the depths of my soul.

indescribable feelings.

when your lips
come alive my world becomes
brighter.
my countenance is elevated,
my eyes excited,
and am caught up
in the glories of you.

when i see you smile
you shine a light in
the atmosphere and
am enthralled by
the magical glow
and sweetness in your smile.

The Seductive Collection

Dewdrops

i'm almost certain
your passionate kisses are
like dewdrops
resting on the petals
of early morning roses,

soft,
sensual,
irresistible,
and
sweet.

i'm pretty confident that
those lips are
as gentle and tender
as dewdrops
slowly kissing
rose petals in
the early morning sunlight.

with lips so seductively alluring
they must feel like
drops of dew romancing
the tender petals
of a blooming rose.

with lips like those
even butterflies
and hummingbirds

r. A. bentinck

must be yearning
to taste their
honeyed sweetness.
i am a rose petal
you can be my dewdrop,
come lay
your affectionate kisses
on me.

The *Seductive* Collection

Watching

you sensed my eyes
gently stroking you
from across the way
and
you intensify your tease
in every little thing you
said and did.

i knew you were aware
that i was staring at you
when you started
to ramp up your sensual meter.

my eyes now transfixed,
my imagination is in
a pulsing blender,

and my mouth is ajar
with extreme anticipation
as you slowly unleash
your fetching heat
bit by bit.

r. A. bentinck

Wordplay

it's the way she gets lost
in her words when she
describe her sensual needs,

it's the way she closes her eyes
when her fertile imagination hits
her sweet spot,

it's the lingering yearnings
she leaves in the core of
your unsatisfied urges.

talking with her
is like having foreplay
with time to spare.

she has the perfect
word combinations.
she stimulates
the imagination and the brain
in unexplainable ways.

she knows what she wants
and she isn't intimidated to express
her feeling unashamedly.

The *Seductive* Collection

Seduction Knocked

seduction knocked
and i opened but
i wasn't prepared for what
she brought with her.

she was draped with
the richest of blessings:

a smile that molested my
excited sensual senses,

eyes that snatch
my breath away
in an instant,

a touch that seeped into
to the core
of my insatiable desires.
seduction knocked
on my heart's door and

i opened up to her
and the unexpected excitements
that she brought left me
speechless.

r. A. bentinck

Pillow Talk

the soothing sound
of your voice is
the perfect dessert
to the intense heat
of our love feast.

your revealing eyes
and your coy smile
doesn't paint a true picture
of your ravishing personality
beneath the sheets.

we are recovering from
an exhausting and
explosive session
of lovemaking by talking
the moments away
as we lay comfortable
and satisfied with each other's
sweaty company.

The Seductive Collection

You Are Too Close

it's the only place
i love to be,
close to you.

it's the only way
i can smell
your sweet fragrance,
when i'm
close to you.

it's the only time
i get the chance
to gaze into your
beautiful brown eyes and
get lost inside of
your dreams,

whenever i'm
close to you.
it's the only moment
i get the opportunity
to bask in the glory of you
when i'm
close you.

you keep telling me
i'm too close to you
but it's the only place i long to be.

r. A. bentinck

Under the Stars

as the evening gradually fades
our closeness takes on
a brand new meaning.
the mellow music in
the background
guide our dancing feet
and fuels our emotions
while we danced under
the watchful eyes
of the twinkling stars.

i hold you close as we dance
the hours away,
i hold you closer and
i can feel your heartbeat
in sync with mine,

i can feel the rhythms of
your fluctuating emotions,
and i can smell
the sweetness of your hair.

as the night swiftly fades
our closeness takes on
new dimensions
that brings us closer together.
and we get lost
in the rhythm of romance.

The *Seductive* Collection

Skin to Skin

there is
a certain magic
when we connect
skin to skin.

there is
explosive beauty
every time we exchange
bodily heat when we are
skin to skin.

there is
unexplained tension
every time your pores
wrestle mine
when we are
skin to skin.
the cares of the world
vanishes whenever
we are
skin to skin.

there is
always magic
when we meet
skin to skin.

r. A. bentinck

The Closer I Get

the closer i get
to you,
the more i see
in you.

the closer i get
to you,
the more i feel
for you.

the closer i get
to you,
the more i want
to be with you.

the closer i get
to you,
the more i get
lost in you.

the closer i get
to you
the more at ease
i feel in your presence.

The Seductive Collection

Let Me

let me take you to
the places you've never
been before.

let me open
the doors to your
undiscovered desires.

let me ignite the fire
of your smouldering yearnings.

and let me arouse
all your
secret fantasies.

r. A. bentinck

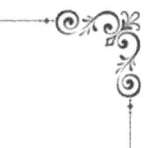

In-between Time

until we meet again
everything seems
to last longer.
the hours seem to drag on,
the days seem like weeks,
and time slows
to a snail's pace.

in-between time
i think of you,
in-between time
i reminisce
about the glorious moments
we've shared,
in-between time
i crave you,
in-between time
i dream about you,

in-between time
i wish on a star
for you.
until we meet again
i will continue to
wish for time
to grow wings and
fly swiftly
until we meet again.

The Seductive Collection

Desperation

she told me
i'm desperate.

desperate
for her to whisper
tantalising words
in my eager ears.

desperate
for her to relax
and sync with
my sensuous rhythm and flow.

desperate
for her to release
her sensual beast
on me and quench
my ever-burning flame.
she is correct
in all instances.

i'm desperate,
but if you see her
and step into my shoes
you won't blame me
for being this way,
because you will
get desperate too.

r. A. bentinck

Overly Excited

maybe one day
you will come
to realise
why am so excited
by you.

maybe if you
just let go.

let go
of your doubts,
let go
of your fears,
and
release your uncertainties,

you too might be
overly excited just like me.
you give me reasons
to be overly excited
about you.

i don't have any apologies
for being excited
by and about you.

The Seductive Collection

Reading Me

she has me figured out.
she can now
read me
like an open book.

she can sense it in
the way i move,
the way i speak,
and
the way i laugh

that i have
an insatiable appetite
for her.

she knows i want
to taste,
and
to explore,
all of her.

and even after all that
i will still want
more
and more
and
more of her.

r. A. bentinck

About The Author

Randy Abubakar Bentinck

Randy Bentinck has several published books. He was very active in the theatre scene in Guyana during the 90s where he acted in many major productions at the Theatre Guild of Guyana and the National Cultural Centre. As a visual artist, he has been a part of several national exhibitions, and his work represented Guyana at Carifesta IX, held in Trinidad and Tobago in 2006.

The Seductive Collection

He has been very active in sports and youth development. He was the chaperone for a youth contingent from Guyana for the first Habitat for Humanity Caribbean Youth Build held in 2000.
'Of all the Lilies' is Bentinck's debut poetry collection published in 2017. This collection features a rich array of poems and prose about various life experiences. Bentinck is originally from the county of Berbice in Guyana but spent most of his adult life in the capital Georgetown.

www.ingramcontent.com/pod-product-compliance
Lightning Source LLC
Chambersburg PA
CBHW032037090426
42744CB00004B/42